REVISED TEACHER'S EDITION

PLAY and PLAY

Piano Book For Beginners

Written by Diane Engle

© 2016, 2021, 2023 by Diane Engle
All rights reserved.
No part of this book may be reproduced in any form or by any electronic or mechanical means, including information storage and retrieval systems, without permission in writing from the author.

dianeengle52@gmail.com
Diane Engle
107 S. Holly Street
DeQuincy, LA 70633
USA

www.dianeenglepianostudio.com

Illustrator: Peggy Condon
Editors: Lindy Robertson and Leslie Engle
Pre-Press Production: Julie Karen Hodgins

PLAY AND PLAY!
Piano Method for Young Beginners

THE METHOD

PLAY AND PLAY! is a unique approach to teaching beginning piano for young students. Piano lessons are taught in a small group setting. Students play singing games then learn to read the music to these singing games on the piano and/or keyboard.

The method is based upon the Kodály philosophy of music instruction, which:
- teaches music literacy;
- progresses from activities through game to song to music symbols for rhythmic and melodic literacy;
- utilizes a child-developmental approach;
- follows the way a child learns, naturally in a step-by-step sequence;
- relates to the child's own development, physically and intellectually; and
- is highly structured and sequenced.

THE SEQUENCE

PLAY AND PLAY! follows the highly sequenced Kodály approach of *Prepare, Present, Practice*.

PREPARE
- Students learn a new music concept through the playing of games, singing of songs, and other activities that have the new concept in them.
- The students are simply *preparing* to learn to read something new in music in a fun way.

PRESENT
- The new music concept is *presented* to the students after they have played the games and sung the songs.
- This will be the first time to actually read the new rhythmic or melodic music concept.
- It is often an easy transition for the students because the concept is familiar to them through the previous lesson when they played the singing game.

PRACTICE
- *Practice* is NOT dull, boring repetition.
- Each concept is introduced and practiced through a variety game songs and activities that excite students.

My personal philosophy of teaching beginning piano in a group setting is, **"Playing games is serious business in piano class!"** *Teaching piano class using this method results in music literacy and is a fun way to teach!*

Diane Engle

Teacher's Edition

THE BENEFITS

STUDENT BENEFITS
- Children learn in a fun setting, with music they can relate to and enjoy playing.
- Singing games make the children want to play the piano.
- Children learn from other students in piano class as well as from the teacher.
- Reinforces the general benefits of music lessons including improvement in child's academic skills. Physical skills are also developed as well as social skills.

PARENT BENEFITS
- Child is motivated to attend weekly lessons in the piano class setting.
- Child is excited to practice at home by, *"playing the game I learned in piano class today!"*

TEACHER BENEFITS
- Teaching hours are consolidated.
- Teacher generates more income in less teaching time.

LESSON FORMAT

TEACHER'S EDITION
- The teacher's edition has the same music page as the student edition to serve as a quick reference in planning and implementing the lesson for the teacher.
- Each lesson plan includes directions to the singing games as well as music instruction.
- Reproducible activities pages are found throughout the teacher edition, as listed in the index.
- Each student page includes a picture to color, allowing the teacher to work with students individually while the others color.

LESSON SEQUENCE
- Each lesson is planned using a 45 minute lesson schedule.
- Lessons can easily be adjusted as needed if more than one class time is needed for the concept being taught.

PIANO CLASS SETTING
- Acoustic piano or digital piano
- Keyboard (61-key keyboard is recommended)
- A white board that includes both blank space and music staves

HANDY DANDY
(not in student book)

This is a fun way to begin piano class. The students will develop a feeling for the steady beat as you say the poem and they will hear an introduction to the difference between high and low sounds.

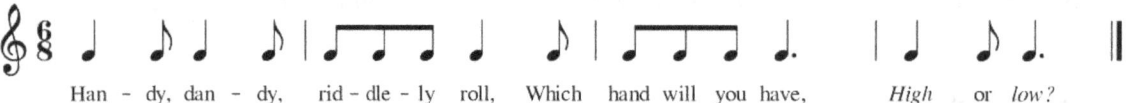

Han - dy, dan - dy, rid - dle - ly roll, Which hand will you have, *High* or *low?*

GAME DIRECTIONS
Object Needed
- Coin or other small object to hide in hand

Have a coin or other small object in one hand. Keep the *steady beat* by moving the object from one hand to the other on the steady beat as you say the poem, keeping the object hidden from the students. Put one closed hand high in the air on the word *"high"*, using a *high* sounding voice on that word. Put the other hand down low by your side on the word *"low"* while using a *low* sounding voice. Keep both hands closed. A student will guess which hand has the object. Say the poem again for each child.

Handy, Dandy,

Rid-dle-ly-roll,

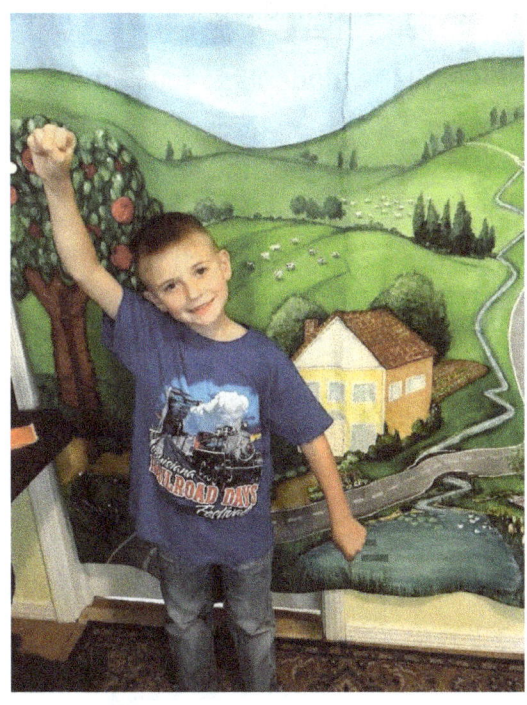

Which hand will you have,

High or low

Play and Play Piano Book for Beginners

I CLIMBED UP THE APPLE TREE

GAME DIRECTIONS
Object Needed
- Hand Drum

Say the poem as you do following motions on each measure:
Measure 1: Step the steady beat.
Measure 2: Both fists on top of head tap the steady beat.
Measure 3: Curve one arm to pretend to be a bowl. Pretend to hold a spoon with the other hand and make a stirring motion.
Measure 4: Point index finger at one child on the steady beat. Student answers yes or no. Say the poem again, giving each student a chance to answer.

MUSIC INSTRUCTIONS
Students say the poem and do motions with you. Instruct the students to do the same motions on the same words as you.
Say the poem again. Touch the apple pictures, keeping a steady beat as the students say the poem and do the motions.
Guide the students to develop an understanding that you were staying steady as you touched the pictures on each row, you stayed *"just the same"* on each row; you did not change and touch faster or slower.
Students will touch apple pictures and say the poem. Instruct the students to touch the same as you, *"just the same."*

HEARTBEAT CHART
Say the poem again as you touch the 16 beat heartbeat chart, page 8. The students will compare the apples page to the heartbeat page. (4 rows, four pictures on each row.)
Define the heart pictures as "heartbeat." *"Heartbeat in music stays the same as you say a poem, sing a song or play the piano/keyboard."*
Play the hand drum as you say the poem.
Students will touch the 16 beat heartbeat chart, student book page 4, and say the poem.

Teacher's Edition

I CLIMBED UP THE APPLE TREE

INSTRUCTIONS
Touch each apple as you say the poem.
Color the apples and the apple tree.

Play and Play Piano Book for Beginners

HEARTBEAT CHART

INSTRUCTIONS
Touch each heartbeat as your teacher plays the drum.
Touch each heartbeat as you say the poem.

FIVE FINGER NUMBERS

INSTRUCTIONS
Help the students trace their hands on page 5 of the student book.
Instruct the students to number the thumb as finger number 1 and fingers 2-5 on each hand.

STUDENT P.5

FIVE FINGER NUMBERS

Trace your hands. Number the fingers.

Right hand

Left hand

Play and Play Piano Book for Beginners

PIANO KEYBOARD

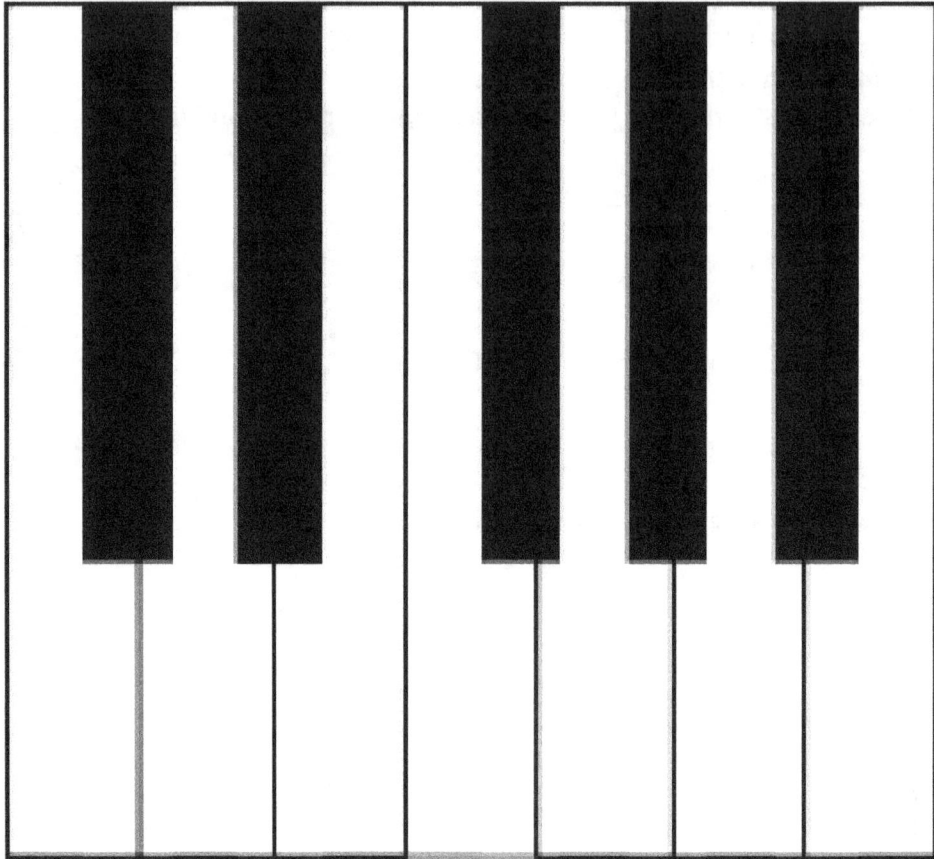

KEYBOARD

TEACHER INSTRUCTIONS

Demonstrate the correct finger and hand position: fingers curved, fingertips on the keys, wrist straight, arms bent at a right angle at the elbow.

BLACK KEY GROUPS: TWO BLACK KEYS

1. Instruct students to look at the black keys and notice the black keys are in different groups. Ask, "How many black keys are in a group?"
2. Instruct students to circle the group of two black keys on the page.
3. Model playing all of the groups of two black keys using fingers 2 and 3 of both hands.
4. Instruct students to follow your model and use fingers 2 and 3 of both hands to play all of the groups of two black keys. They will start with the left hand then change to the right hand when they get to the middle of the keyboard.

BLACK KEY GROUPS: THREE BLACK KEYS

1. Instruct students to circle the group of three black keys on the page.
2. Model playing all of the groups of three black keys using fingers 2, 3, and 4 of both hands.
3. Instruct students to follow your model and use fingers 2, 3, and 4 of both hands to play all of the groups of three black keys. They will start with the left hand then change to the right hand when they get to the middle of the keyboard.

PIANO KEYBOARD

INSTRUCTIONS
Circle the two black key group.
Find a group of two black keys on the keyboard with your left hand. Use fingers 2 and 3 to play the black keys in the two black key group.
Find a group of two black keys on the keyboard with your right hand. Use fingers 2 and 3 to play the black keys in the two black key group.

Circle the three black key group.
Find a group of three black keys on the keyboard with your left hand. Use fingers 2, 3, and 4 to play the black keys in the three black key group.
Find a group of three black keys on the keyboard with your right hand. Use fingers 2, 3, and 4 to play the black keys in the three black key group.

Play and Play Piano Book for Beginners

IN AND OUT

In and out, 'Round a-bout, O - U - T and that spells out!

TEACHER INSTRUCTIONS
Play the game before introducing the song on the piano/keyboard.

GAME INSTRUCTIONS
Objects Needed
- Beanbag for passing on the steady beat.
- Rhythm sticks
- Hand drum

Touch the heartbeat chart on page 8 as you sing the song. Guide the students to discover the silent heartbeats on rows 1, 2, and 4 of the chart. Students will touch the heartbeat chart on page 4 in their book as they listen to you sing again. The students will sing the song and touch the heartbeat chart. Remind the students of the silent heartbeats.

Students stand in a circle and pass the bean bag to the person on the right on the beat as they sing. Remind students that the bean bag continues to be passed on the silent heartbeat. The person who has the bean bag on the last beat of the song is "out". That person will get out of the circle and get a rhythm instrument to keep the beat as the game continues. As each person is out, the circle closes up their place. The winner is the last person remaining without being "out."

PIANO/KEYBOARD INSTRUCTIONS
Review the groups of two and three black keys. Students place left hand on a group of two black keys and right hand on a group of three black keys. Guide the students to play with right hand when the finger number 2 is high above the bean bag picture and with left hand when finger number 2 is below the bean bag picture. The students will nod their head for the silent heartbeat on lines 1, 2, and 4.

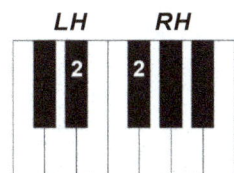

IN AND OUT

INSTRUCTIONS
Put your right hand finger 2 on the group of **three** black keys. Put your left hand finger 2 on the group of **two** black keys. Play with your right hand when finger 2 is above the bean bag. Play with your left hand when finger 2 is below the bean bag.
The heartbeat with no picture means a silent heartbeat. Do not play. Just nod your head on the silent heartbeat.
Play and sing the words.
Color the bean bags.

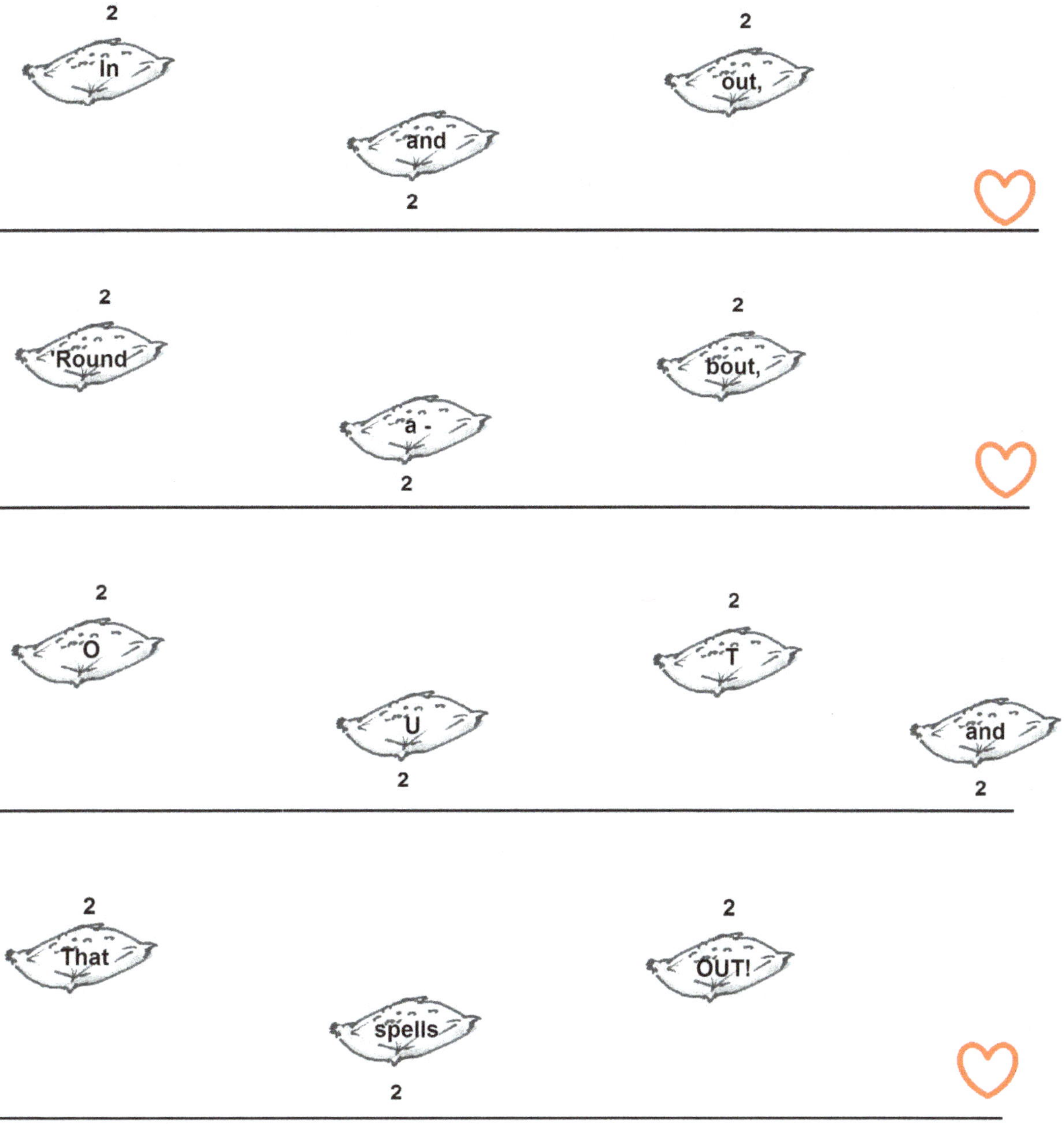

2 — In
2 — and
2 — out,
♥

2 — Round
2 — a-
2 — bout,
♥

2 — O
2 — U
2 — T
2 — and

2 — That
2 — spells
2 — OUT!
♥

Play and Play Piano Book for Beginners

BLACK KEY SONGS

TEACHER INSTRUCTIONS
Sing the songs and play the game before introducing the songs on the piano/keyboard. Touch the two row heartbeat chart as you sing the song.

GAME INSTRUCTIONS
Sing each song as you name it in the story.
Story: *Snails love the flower garden. They also love the rain because the rain makes the flowers grow. Let's pretend we are the snail in the garden and we are going 'round and 'round.*
CIRCLE GAME: Teacher and students join hands to walk in a circle as they sing.
SNAIL SHELL GAME: Teacher and students join hands to form a straight line. The teacher is the line leader. The student at the end of the line stands still as the teacher leads the line around the student to wind the line into the snail shell.

PIANO/KEYBOARD INSTRUCTIONS
Students place left hand on a group of 2 black keys and right hand on a group of three black keys. Guide the students to play with right hand when finger number 2 is above the picture and with left hand when finger 2 is below the picture.

Teacher's Edition

SNAIL, SNAIL

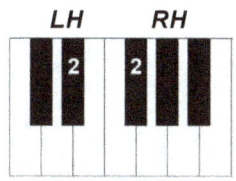

INSTRUCTIONS
Put your right hand finger 2 on the group of three black keys.
Put your left hand finger 2 on the group of two black keys.
Play and sing the finger numbers.
Play and sing the words. Your teacher will help you sing the words under the under the snail picture.

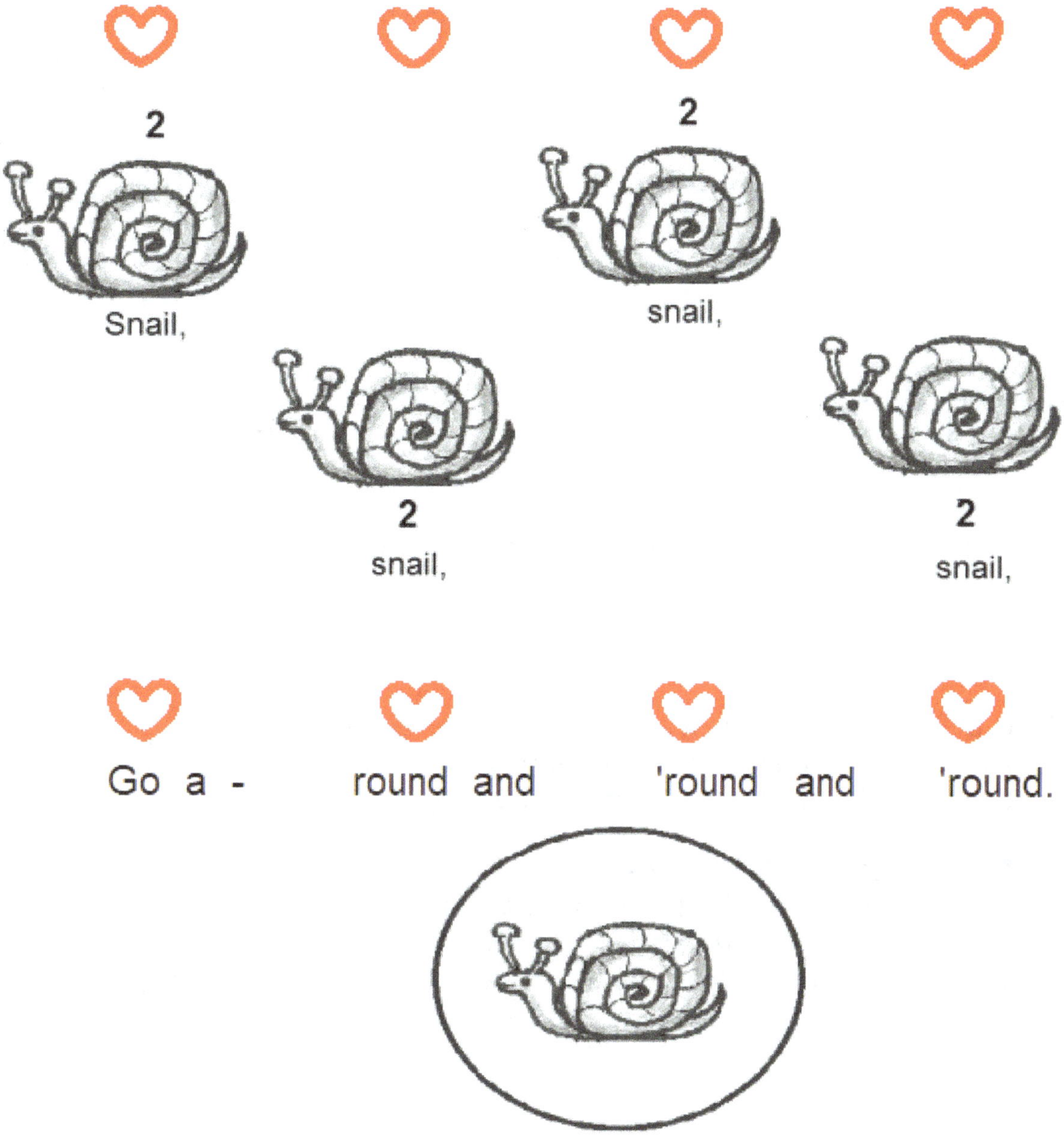

♡ ♡ ♡ ♡

2   2

Snail,   snail,

2   2

snail,   snail,

♡ ♡ ♡ ♡

Go a -   round and   'round and   'round.

Play and Play Piano Book for Beginners

BOUNCE HIGH

TEACHER INSTRUCTIONS
Sing the song and play the game before the students play the music on the piano/keyboard. Touch the heartbeat pictures as you sing the song.

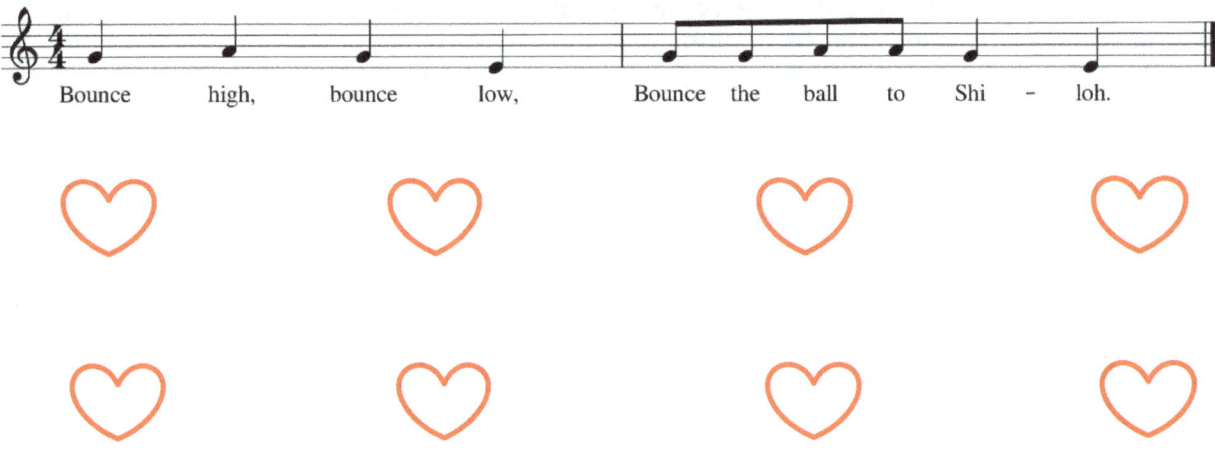

GAME DIRECTIONS
Object Needed
- Large Ball

Students stand in a circle. Teacher stands in the middle of the circle and bounces the ball to each child as the song is sung. Student bounces the ball back to the teacher.

Variations:
- Students bounce the ball to next student around the circle.
- Two students bounce the ball back and forth to each other.
- Student bounces the ball alone throughout the song.

PIANO/KEYBOARD INSTRUCTIONS
Students will use same hand position as in "Snail, Snail" and "Rain, Rain." Instruct the students that they will also play finger 3 in right hand. Students will touch the words located at the bottom of the page as they sing all of the song.

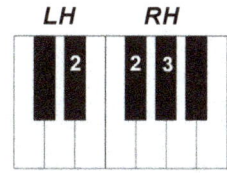

BOUNCE HIGH

INSTRUCTIONS

Put your right hand on a group of three black keys.
Put your left hand on a group of two black keys.
Play and sing the finger numbers.
Remember to play with your right hand when the finger numbers are above the picture and with your left hand when the finger numbers are below the picture.
Play and sing the words.

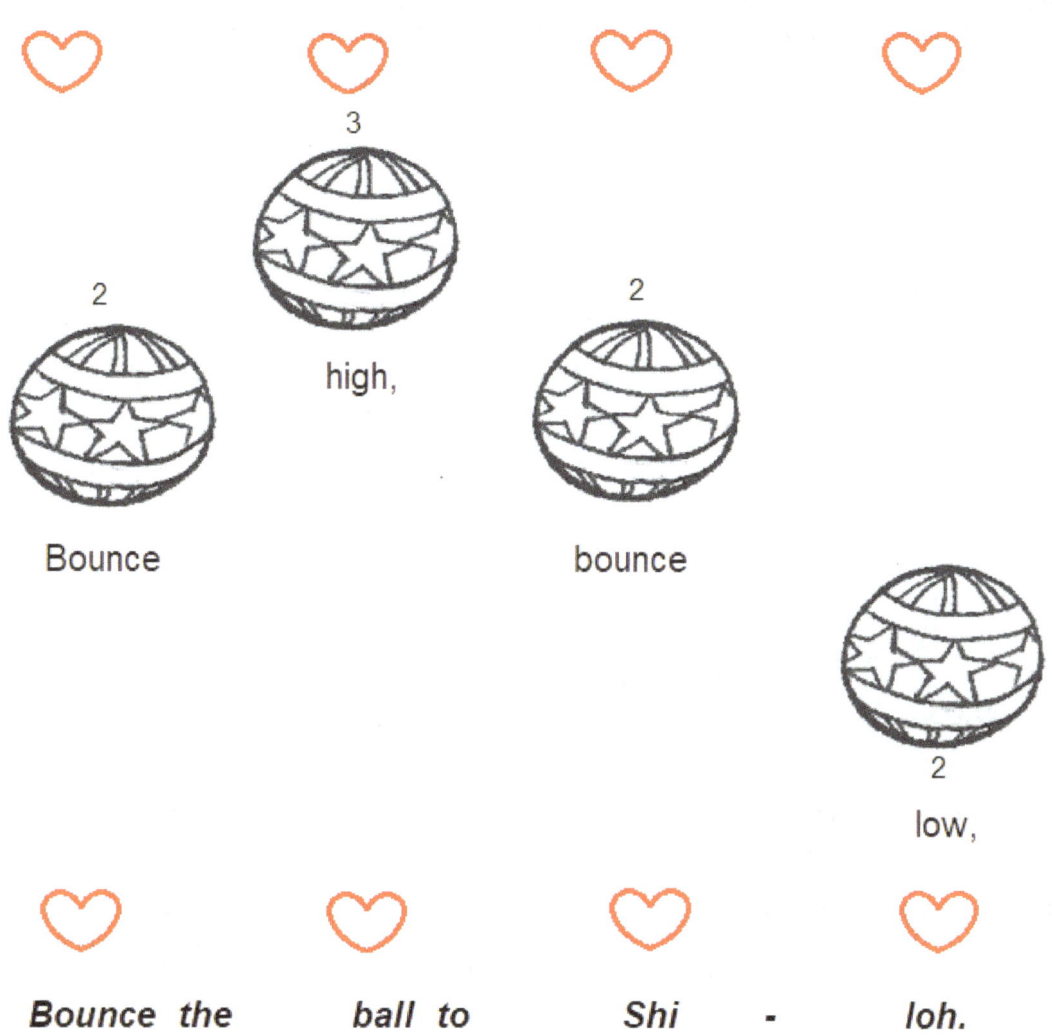

APPLE, PEACH, PEAR, PLUM

GAME DIRECTIONS
Objects Needed
- **Hand drum or rhythm sticks**

Tap the rhythm of the poem on the drum as the students say the poem.* Guide the students to develop an understanding that you tapped all of the sounds of the poem and that you tapped *"the way the words go."* Each student taps the rhythm and says the poem as the other students touch the pictures of the poem. Remind students to touch each picture *"the way the words go."* Students tell their birthday.

Touch each picture and say the words *"long"* and *"short-short"* to match the pictures under the heartbeats. The words *"long"* and *"short-short"* represent the rhythm sounds for each beat. Students will touch the pictures and say *"long"* and *"short-short"* in place of the words of the poem.

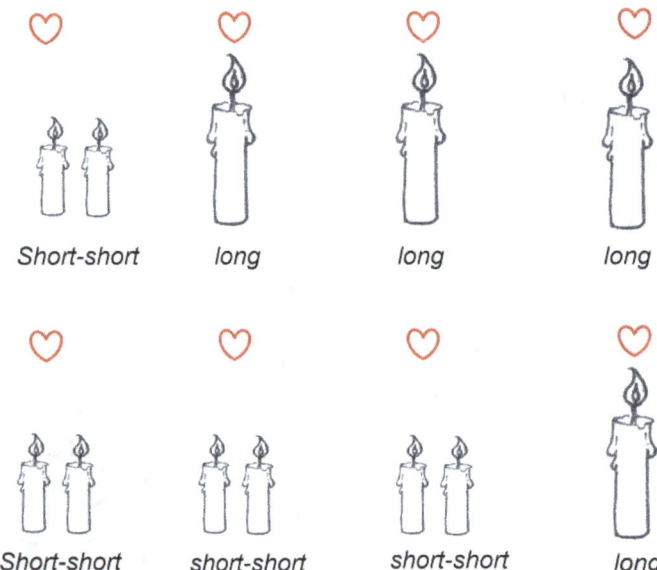

Guide the students to develop an understanding that there is one sound under the heartbeat for the *"long"* sound and there are two sounds under the heartbeat for the *"short-short"* sounds.

*The pictures under the heartbeats in this poem and upcoming poems and songs are sized to represent the rhythm. The one bigger picture under the heartbeat represents the quarter note in two beat or four beat meter. The two smaller pictures under one heartbeat represent two eighth notes in two beat or four beat meter.

APPLE, PEACH, PEAR, PLUM

INSTRUCTIONS
Say the poem and clap the way the words go.
Touch the pictures and say the poem. Be sure to touch each picture.
Touch the pictures and say the long and short-short sounds.
Clap and say the long and short-short sounds.

Ap · ple,   peach,   pear,   plum;

Tell me   when your   birth- day   comes.

Play and Play Piano Book for Beginners

STUDENT P.11

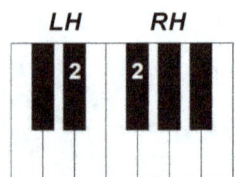

RAIN, RAIN

INSTRUCTIONS
Clap and read the long and short-short sounds.
Put your right hand finger 2 on a group of three black keys.
Put your left hand finger 2 on a group of two black keys.
Play with your right hand when 2 is above the raindrop picture.
Play with your left hand when 2 is below the raindrop picture.
Play and sing the long and short-short sounds then play and sing the words.
Touch your head with your fingertips as you sing the bottom line of words.

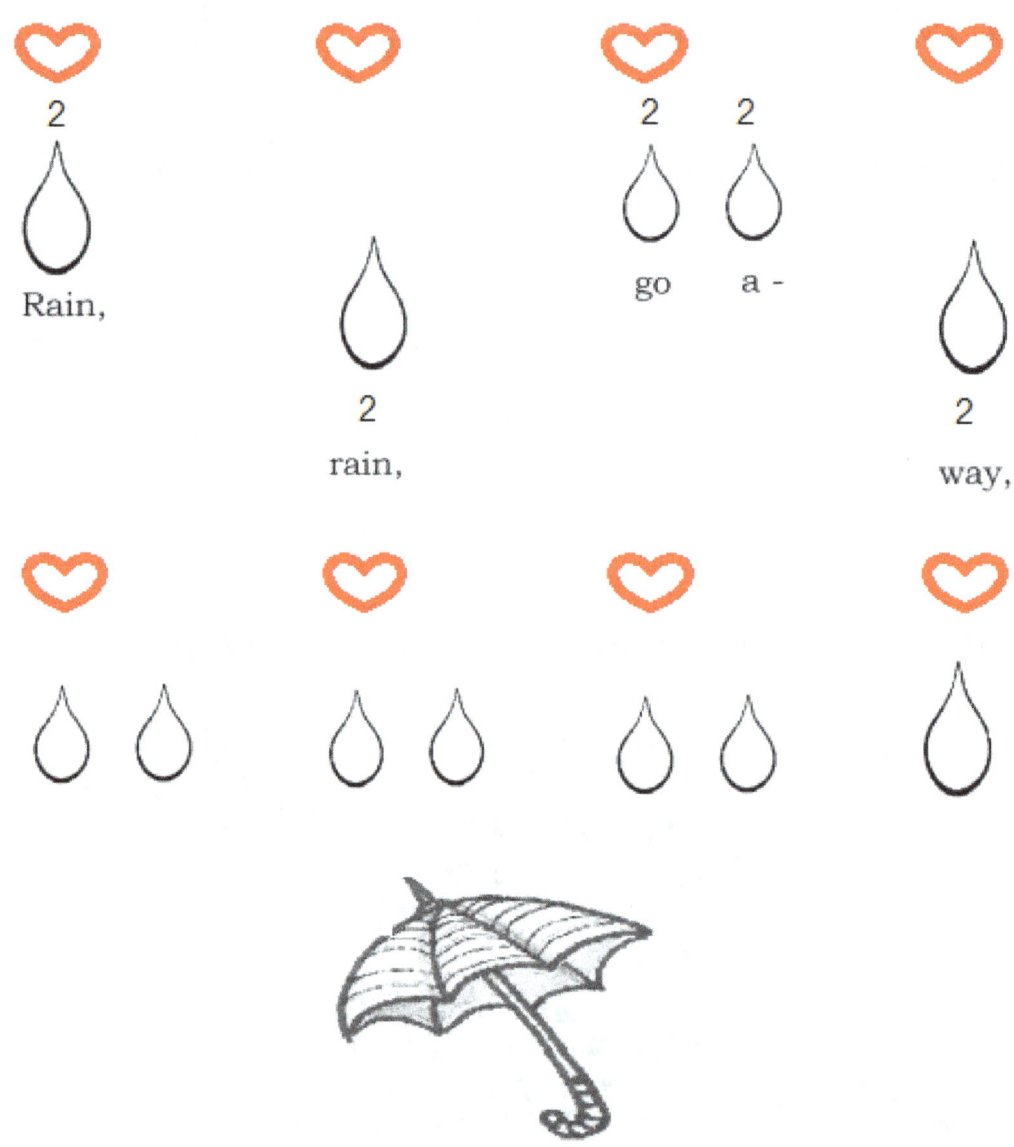

20 Teacher's Edition

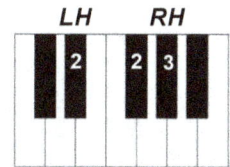

BOUNCE HIGH

INSTRUCTIONS
Touch the pictures and say the long and short-short sounds.
Clap and read the long and short-short sounds.
Put your right hand on the group of three black keys.
Put your left hand on the group of two black keys.
Play and sing the long and short-short sounds then play and sing the words.

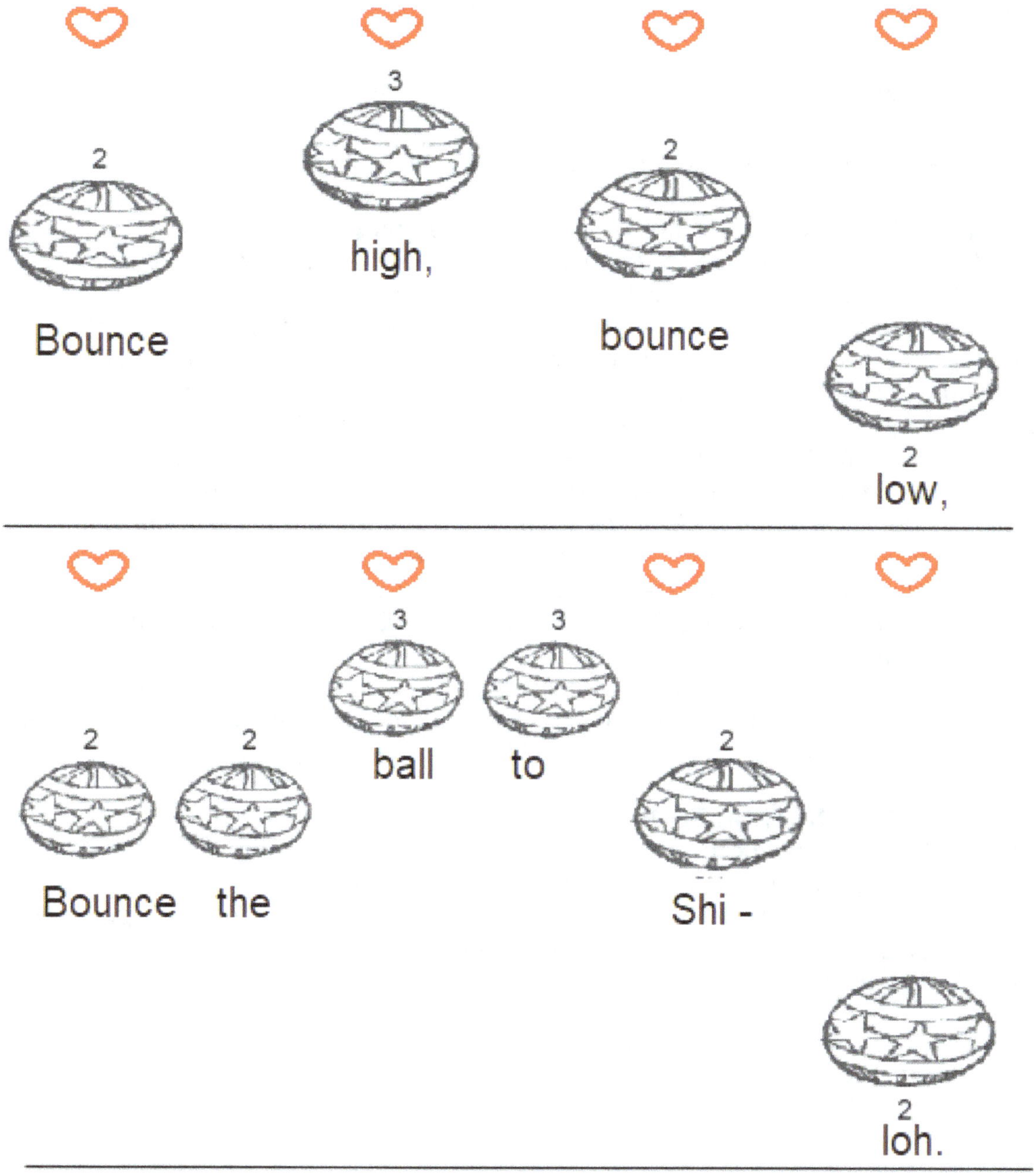

Bounce high, bounce low,

Bounce the ball to Shi - loh.

Play and Play Piano Book for Beginners

LUCY LOCKET

TEACHER INSTRUCTIONS
Sing the song and play the game before the students play the music on the piano/keyboard.

GAME DIRECTIONS
Object Needed
- small wallet with ribbon tied around it or picture of wallet with ribbon

Tell the story of Lucy Locket to introduce the game song.
One day Lucy Locket was walking to the bakery. She had her small wallet called a "pocket" with her. She passed many things on her way to the bakery and sometimes stopped to talked to friends. When she got to the bakery she realized that her pocket was missing. "Oh, no!," she said, "I have lost my pocket. I know I had it when I left the house. I must have dropped it along the way. I will walk back the same way and see if I can find it." Lucy Locket's friend, Kitty Fisher helped her find it. Our singing voices will be Kitty Fisher. When Lucy is walking and looking for her pocket and she is far away from it, we will sing with our soft voices. Lucy will know that the pocket is far away and will keep walking. When Lucy Locket is close to her pocket we will sing with our loud voices. Lucy will stop and look around whenever she hears our loud voices because she knows she is close to her pocket. Remember to use your pretty singing voice whenever you sing loudly. That is called "FORTE" in music. Our soft voice is called "PIANO", the same word as our piano musical instrument.
Choose a student to be Lucy Locket. Lucy hides his/her eye while you hide the wallet. Give the student a specific path to follow around the room as he/she looks for the wallet.

PIANO/KEYBOARD INSTRUCTIONS
Students will follow the instructions as given on their song sheet. Demonstrate the technique of playing loud and soft, defining the terms *forte* and *piano*.
A challenge for students: *"Play the song from memory. Play the song forte and piano as you watch Lucy Locket look for her pocket. Your loud and soft playing will help Lucy Locket find her pocket."*

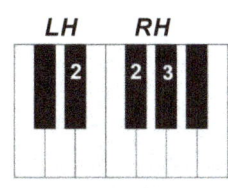

LUCY LOCKET

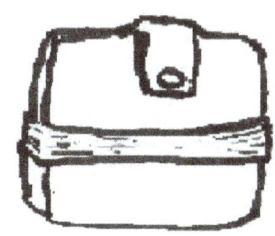

INSTRUCTIONS
Clap and read the long and short-short sounds.
Put your right hand on a group of three black keys and your left hand on a group of two black keys.
Play and sing the finger numbers then play and sing the long and short-short sounds.
Play and sing the words.

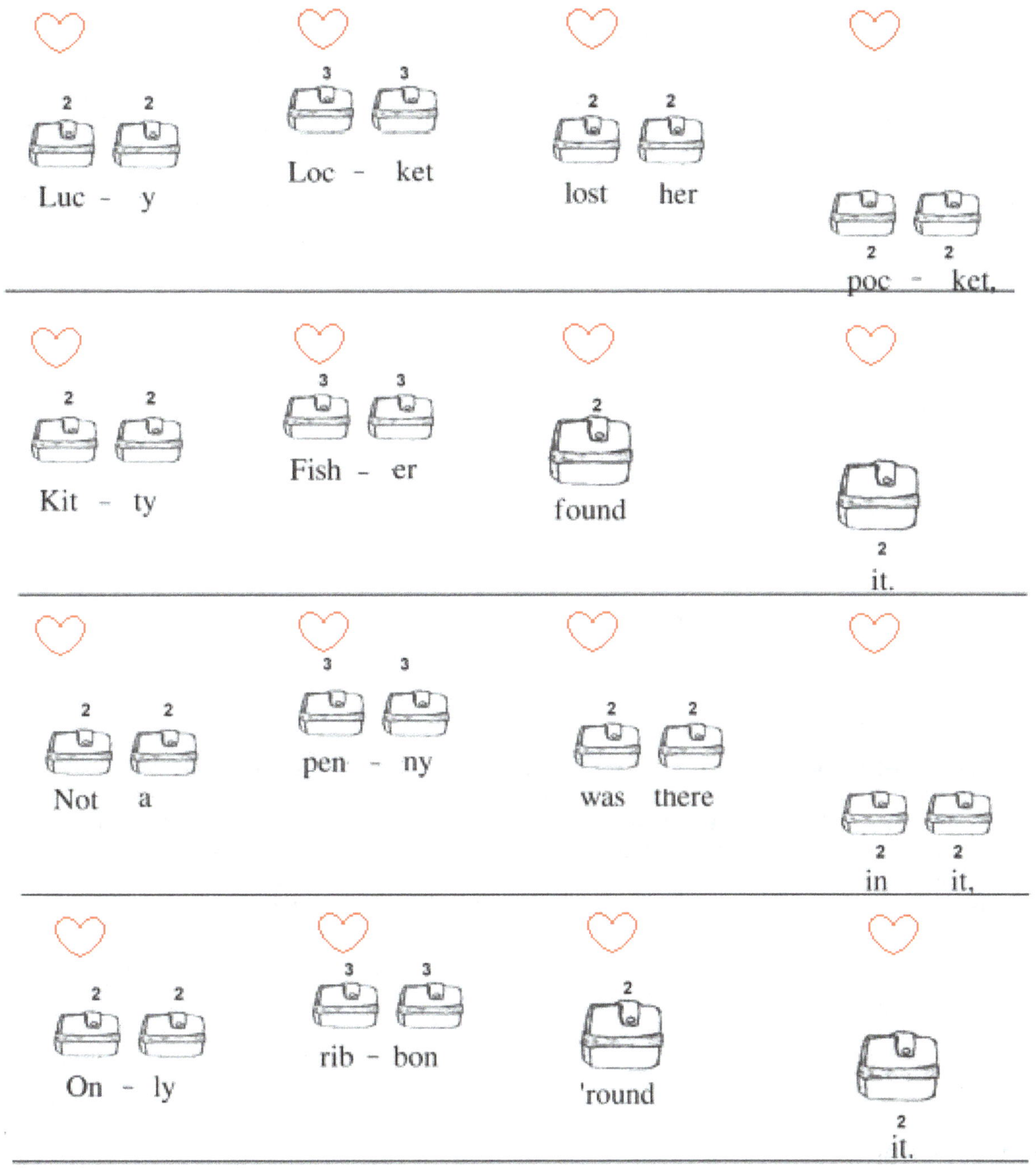

Luc - y   Loc - ket   lost   her   poc - ket,

Kit - ty   Fish - er   found   it.

Not   a   pen - ny   was   there   in   it,

On - ly   rib - bon   'round   it.

Play and Play Piano Book for Beginners

RHYTHM

Quarter Note and Eighth Notes in 2/4 Meter
Meter Signature

TEACHER INSTRUCTIONS
Materials needed:
- *Pages 10-13 in the student book*
- *Copy of page 10 in the student book*

Students sing the songs found on these pages 11-13. Choose one of the singing games to play.

Students touch the pictures as they sing the songs. Students sing again and clap as they sing. Remind students that they are clapping *"the way the words go."*

Students touch the pictures and say the *"long, short-short"* names for the songs on pages 11-13. see the example using *"Rain, Rain"* below. (the same Rain, Rain music is inserted below this.)

Return to the poem, *"Apple, Peach, Pear, Plum"*, page 10. Have the students clap and say the *"long, short-short"* patterns as you draw vertical lines on the pictures of the candles, using the copy.

Connect the *short-short* lines with a beam across the top. Name the lines as *the rhythm,* which means the sounds on each beat. Name the *long* sound *ta* (pronounced tah) and the *short-short* sounds *ti-ti* (pronounced with long e sound). Students will draw the lines and beams on their page then touch and read the rhythm. Tell the students, *"This is a shortcut way to write the rhythm. Musicians name the ta quarter note and the ti's eighth notes. They add noteheads to the bottom and shade them in."* Draw the noteheads and shade them in. Guide the students to do the same.

MUSIC DIRECTIONS
Guide the students to discover the music on their page 14. The students will follow instructions as given. Remind the students that they will say the *"ta"* and *"ti-ti"* names as they read the rhythm.

APPLE, PEACH, PEAR, PLUM

INSTRUCTIONS
Touch each heartbeat as you say the poem.
Touch each word or part of the word as you say the poem.
Clap the rhythm as you say the poem. Remember, the rhythm is *"the way the words go."*
Clap and read the rhythm names.

Ap - ple, peach, pear, plum;

Tell me when your birth - day comes.

Play and Play Piano Book for Beginners

BEE, BEE, BUMBLEBEE

STEADY BEAT GAME DIRECTIONS
Objects Needed
Picture of bumblebee or hand puppet
16 Beat Heartbeat Chart

Have students sit in a circle. Say the poem as you go around the circle, tapping each student on the beat. On the word, *"out",* the student who was touched *"gets out of the circle"* and find a new place to sit in the room. Say the poem again until all students are seated in a new place in the room.

The students will touch the 16 beat heartbeat chart as they say the poem.

RHYTHM GAME DIRECTIONS
Objects Needed
Picture of bumblebee for each student
Bouquet of artificial flowers to represent flower garden

The students say the poem and clap the rhythm, *"the way the words go."* Each student holds a bumblebee picture and touches a flower to the rhythm of the poem.

The students touch the notes and read the rhythm.

BEE, BEE, BUMBLEBEE

INSTRUCTIONS
Touch each heartbeat as you say the poem.
Touch each word or part of the word as you say the poem.
Clap the rhythm as you say the poem. Remember, the rhythm is *"the way the words go."*
Clap and read the rhythm note names.

Bee, Bee, Bum - ble Bee,

Stung a man up - on his knee.

Stung a pig up - on his snout.

I de - clare if you aren't out!

Play and Play Piano Book for Beginners

PEASE PORRIGE HOT
QUARTER REST

TEACHER INSTRUCTIONS
Say the poem and play the game before students read and play the music. Lines 3 and 4 of the poem are not written in the student book.

GAME DIRECTIONS Two students face each other.
 Steady beat motions:
 *clap hands
 + pat both partner's hands,
 ^ one student hold arms in a circle shape in front to represent the pot while the other student pretends to stir with a large spoon in the pot.

```
*    +    *    +    *    +    *    +
```
Pease porridge hot,   Pease porridge cold,

^

Pease porridge in the pot, nine days old.

```
*    +    *    +    *    +    *    +
```
Some like it hot,   Some like it cold,

^

Some like it in the pot nine days old.

Say the poem again with partners changing pot/spoon stirring motion.

MUSIC DIRECTIONS
Students will pat the beat and say the poem. Students will touch the words as they say the poem. Guide the students to touch the empty place in the word lines when there is a silent beat.
Name the *rest* music symbol that is above the empty place in the word line. Guide the students to develop an understanding that rest equals one silent heartbeat.

Students touch the music and read the rhythm. Remind students to be silent on the *rest*. Students clap and read the rhythm. Have the students touch shoulders silently on the silent beat, rest.

PEASE PORRIDGE HOT

INSTRUCTIONS
Pat the beat as you read the words.
Clap the rhythm as you read the words. Remember, the rest is a silent beat.
Clap and read the rhythm note names.

Pease	por- ridge	hot,	(rest)
Pease	por- ridge	cold.	(rest)
Pease	por- ridge	in the	pot,
Nine	days	old.	(rest)

Play and Play Piano Book for Beginners

CLOSET KEY
Meter Signature

TEACHER INSTRUCTIONS
Sing the song and play the game before students read and play the music on the piano/keyboard.

GAME DIRECTIONS
Objects Needed:
- Green old fashioned skeleton key made of sturdy material or a real key painted green.
- Flower garden picture or silk flowers and greenery pasted to poster board.

Tell the story to introduce the game song.
One day someone just your age was walking to town with Mother. Mother stopped suddenly, turned to her child and said, "Oh dear! I forgot to lock the closet. There is something very important in it! I am going to give you the key. You are old enough to walk home by yourself and lock the closet. Then come straight back and meet me at the bakery." The child took the key and started back home. On the way, he had to pass a beautiful flower garden in the neighbor lady's front yard. He stopped to look and accidentally dropped the closet key! It was hard to find because the key was green, just like the grass and stems and leaves of the flowers. The lady saw him drop the key and said, "I will help. You stand here at the garden gate and just look all around for it. Do not walk in the garden. You can point when you see the key and I will get it for you."

One student hides his/her eyes while the teacher or another student "hides" the green key in the flower garden with just a small part of the key showing. The teacher and the other students sing the song as the student stands behind a child representing the garden gate and looks for the key. The teacher is the "lady/gentleman of the garden." Once the student spots the key, the teacher picks up the key. The game continues as each student has a turn to look for the key.

PIANO/KEYBOARD INSTRUCTIONS
This song introduces the meter signature, bar lines, measure and double bar line.

Identify $\heartsuit$ with a **2** above it as the symbol that tells that the heartbeats are in groups of 2. Identify the bar lines as the lines that separate the heartbeats into groups of 2. Identify the measures as the area between the bar lines where the notes are written. Identify the double bar line as the symbol placed at the end of the song.

Guide the students to touch the heartbeats and identify 2 beats in each measure.

Guide the students to identify the skip from finger 2 to finger 4. Remind students that they will skip a black key as they skip finger 3. Guide the students to identify the steps with fingers 4-3-2 in the last measure.

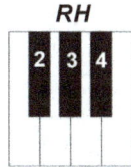 RH

CLOSET KEY

INSTRUCTIONS
Touch the heartbeats and read the rhythm.
Touch the notes and read the rhythm.
Clap and read the rhythm.
Put your right hand on the group of three black keys.
Play and sing the finger numbers.
Play and sing the rhythm names then play and sing the words.

 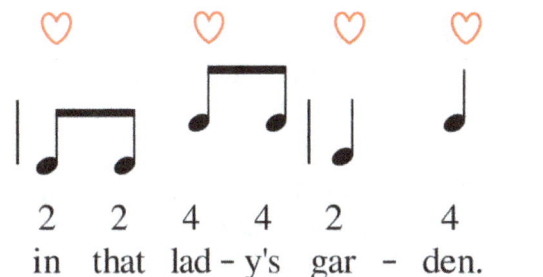

2 2 4 4 2 2 4   2 2 4 4 2   4
I have lost the clo-set key,   in that lad-y's gar - den.

 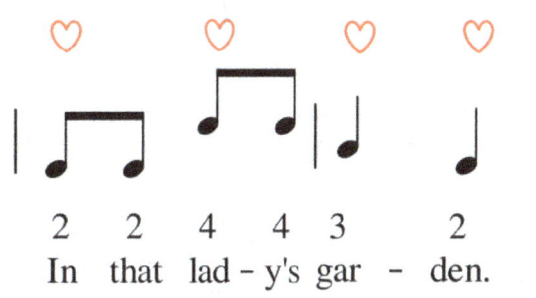

2 2 4 4 2 2 4   2 2 4 4 3   2
I have lost the clo-set key,   In that lad-y's gar - den.

Play and Play Piano Book for Beginners

FROG IN THE MEADOW

TEACHER INSTRUCTIONS

Sing the song and play the game before students read and play the music on the piano/keyboard.

Frog in the mea-dow, can't get him out. Take a lit-tle stick, and stire him a-bout!
(Spoken) *Leap, leap, leap, down!*

GAME DIRECTIONS

Objects Needed
- small stick or mallet to use as "stirrer"

Leapfrog Version

Four students squat on the floor in a straight line. Once down on the floor, they "hide in the meadow" by putting knees and head on the floor, arms over their heads. The teacher taps the last child in line on the back with the stick on the words, *"take a little stick and stir him about"*. The last child stands, spreads legs, puts hands on back of each child in row in front of him as he leaps over them on the words, *"leap, leap, leap"*; then goes down to hide again in the front on the word, *"down."*

The Stirrer and the Frog Version

Students are scattered about the room, squatting on the floor. They "hide in the meadow" by putting knees and head on the floor, arms over their heads. One child is the "Stirrer" of the frogs. The student holds the stick and closes his/her eyes while the teacher chooses one of the frogs to be "It". The "Stirrer" opens eyes, walks among the frogs and sings, pretending to stir the frogs by moving stick in a circle in the air as he/she walks and sings. On the words, *"leap, leap, leap, down"*, all the frogs leap three times in any direction they choose, then hide back down. The student who is "It" immediately gets back up to leap and try to catch the "Stirrer". "Stirrer" is caught if the frog touches his foot or leg. Only the frog selected as "It" attempts to catch the "Stirrer." The frog can only chase the "Stirrer" by leaping.

PIANO/KEYBOARD INSTRUCTIONS

Guide the students to understand that the stems of the notes are drawn down on the left side of the noteheads. This indicates they will play the song with their left hand. Students will follow instructions as given on their song sheet.

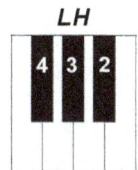

FROG IN THE MEADOW

INSTRUCTIONS
Touch the heartbeats and read the rhythm.
Touch the notes and read the rhythm.
Clap and read the rhythm.
Put your left hand on the group of three black keys.
Play and sing the finger numbers.
Play and sing the rhythm names then play and sing the words.

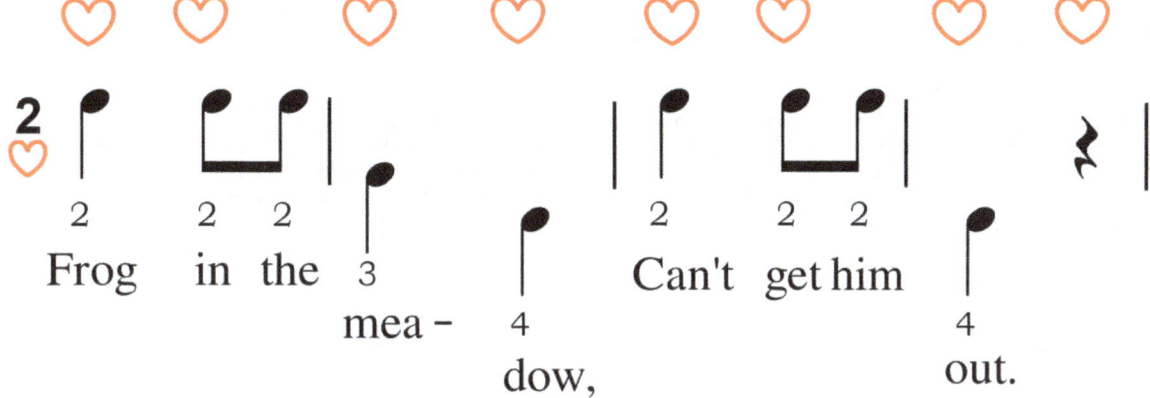

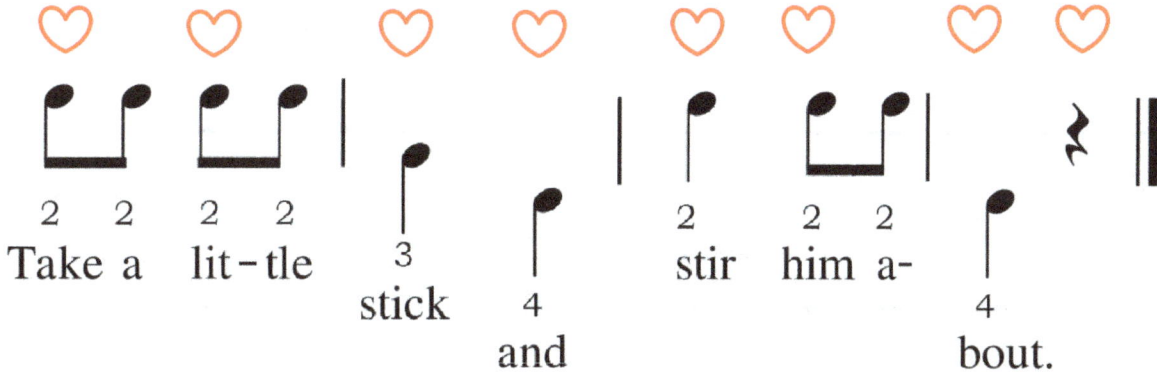

Play and Play Piano Book for Beginners

FLASHCARDS

All of these 4 beat rhythm patterns are taken from songs and rhymes that the students have read. They are to be copied and used for various activities during piano class such as practice, review, memory work, etc. See suggestions below.

Hold up cards one at a time. Students read and clap each rhythm pattern. Guide the students to understand that the red dots represent the steady beat.

Each student has a copy of the flashcards to use for various activities:
  * Put all the cards where they can see each card. Clap and say a pattern. Students listen, echo clap and say the pattern, then hold up the correct card. You may want to select 4 of the cards the first time you do this activity.
  * Clap a pattern without reading it. Students echo clap and say the pattern then hold up the correct card.
  * Students take turns clapping a pattern for the other students to echo and identify.

CLAP WHAT YOU DON'T SEE GAME
Hold up a card, then turn it down where the students cannot see it. Students clap and say the pattern.
Another day, while the students are clapping the first card, hold up a second card for them to see as they are clapping. Students immediately clap the second card after completely the 4 beat pattern of the first card.
Challenge: Go through all 8 cards as described above. The goal is for the students to keep the steady beat throughout and clap each card from memory.

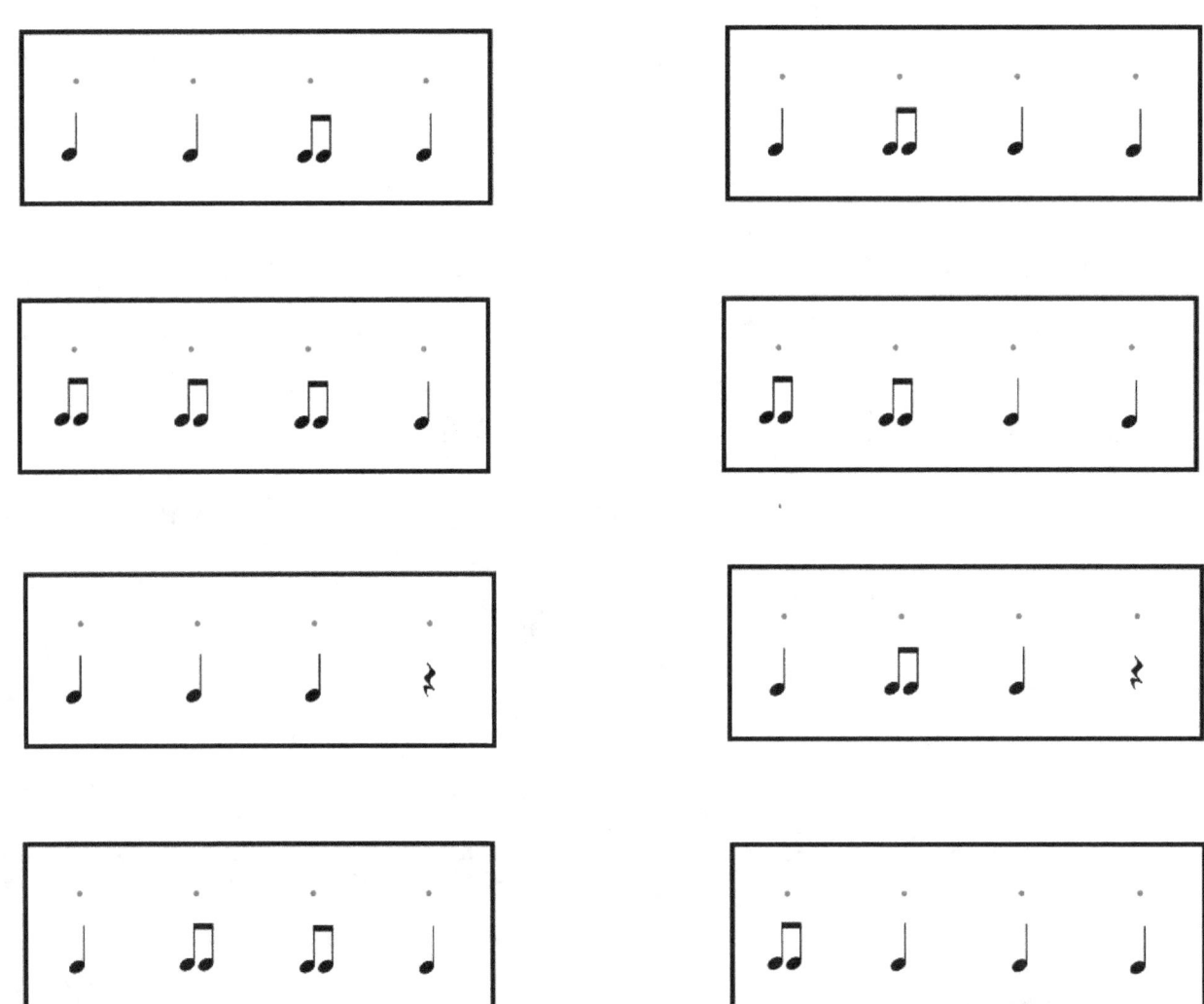

Teacher's Edition

MUSIC ALPHABET

TEACHER INSTRUCTIONS

Students read the letters of the music alphabet, **A B C D E F G**. Play all the white keys of the keyboard and have the students say the note names with you. They can also take turns playing and saying the note names after you have played up through Middle C.

Guide the students to follow the instructions on student book p. 19 to discover the *F* white key location in relation to the group of three black keys and the *D* white key location in relation to the group of two black keys.

Students play F above middle C with their fourth finger. Students play D above middle C with their second finger.

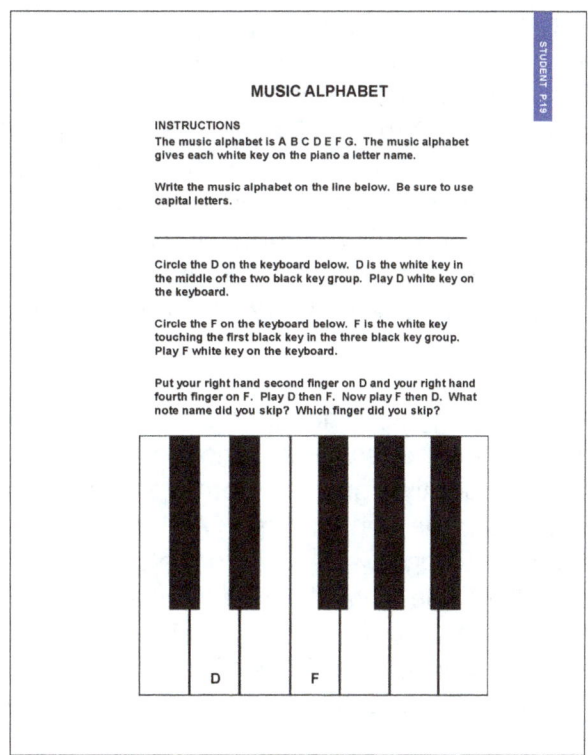

PIANO/KEYBOARD INSTRUCTIONS

Guide the students to discover they will play the familiar song, *"Doggie, Doggie"* on the F and D white keys.

Guide the students to find F on the piano/keyboard. Show the students that F is the first white key touching the group of three black keys and that D is the white key in the middle of the group of two black keys. Guide the students to discover F down to D is a skip and they will skip one white key.

DOGGIE, DOGGIE

TEACHER INSTRUCTIONS
Sing the song and play the game before students read and play the music on the piano/keyboard.

GAME DIRECTIONS
Objects Needed
- Bone, plastic or cardboard
- Chair to represent doghouse.

Tell the story to introduce the game song.
Doggie belonged to a nice family They had a dog house for Doggie and remembered to keep water in a bowl and to feed Doggie every day. Doggie loved to run and play in the meadow. One day Doggie saw a bone in the grass. Doggie thought, "I will take this bone to my dog house and chew on it." About that time, Doggie heard the family call to come eat. Doggie ran to the doghouse, and saw his bowl full of food. He ate all the food, drank all the water, then thought, "Oh my, I'm too full right now to chew on the bone that I found. I will save it 'til later, after I take a nap in my doghouse." While Doggie was asleep, another dog sneaked up and grabbed the bone. We must let Doggie know.

Select one student to be "Doggie." The student will place the bone under the chair, sit in the chair with back to the other students, and close eyes, pretending to be asleep. When you begin singing, silently signal to another student to go get the bone, go back to their place and hide the bone behind them. All the other students should also hide hands behind their back. "Doggie" sings, *"who stole my bone"*, keeping eyes closed. The student who stole the bone sings, "*I stole your bone.*" "Doggie turns around and guesses who stole the bone.
Alternate reply from student who stole bone: The student makes a dog sound, barking, whimpering, growling, etc., instead of singing, *"I stole your bone."*

PIANO/KEYBOARD INSTRUCTIONS
Students will read and clap the rhythm then clap and sing the song.
Students will touch and sing the letter names.
Guide the students to find F on the piano/keyboard. Show the students that F is the first white key touching the group of three black keys and that D is the white key in the middle of the group of two black keys. Guide the students to discover F down to D is a skip and they will skip one white key.

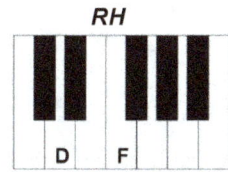

DOGGIE, DOGGIE

INSTRUCTIONS
Clap and read the rhythm.
Put finger 4 of your right hand on the F white key. F white key touches the first black key in the group of 3 black keys.
Finger 2 will play the D white key. D white key is found in between the black keys of the 2 black key group. Play and sing the letter names.
Play and sing the rhythm names then play and sing the words.

Dog - gie,   Dog - gie,   where's your   bone?

Some-one   stole it   from your   home!

Who   stole my   bone?

Play and Play Piano Book for Beginners

STUDENT P.21

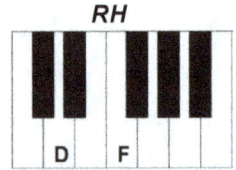

IN AND OUT

INSTRUCTIONS
Clap and read the rhythm.
Put finger 4 of your right hand on the F white key.
Finger 2 will play the D white key.
Play and sing the note names then play and sing the words.

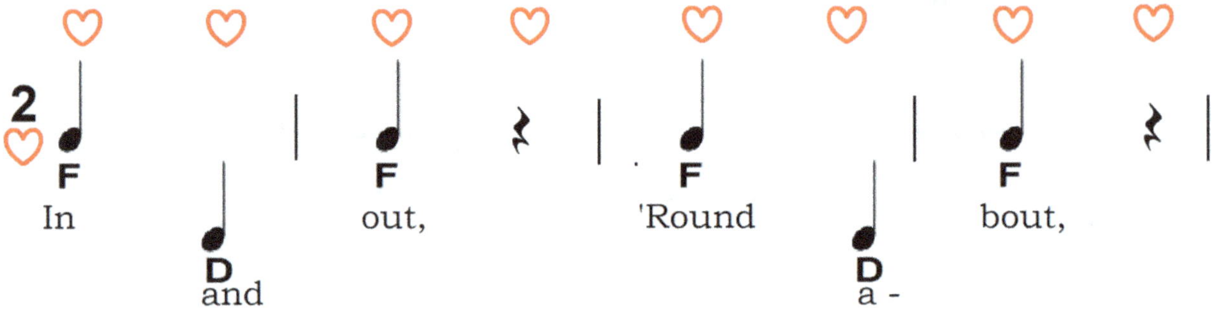

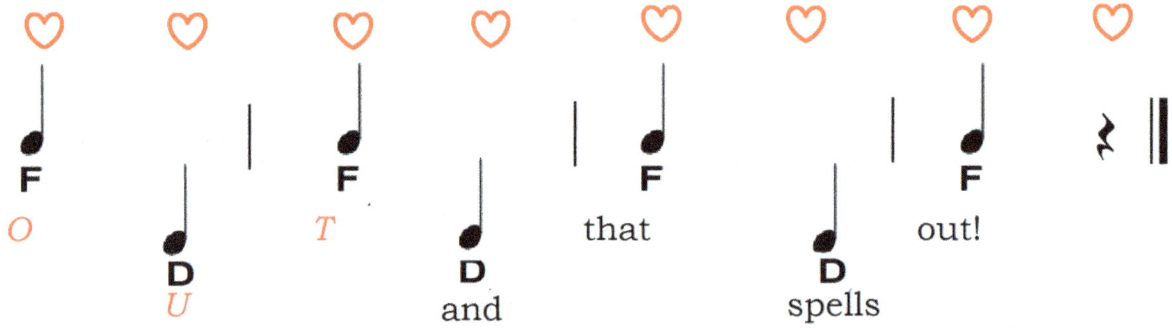

F	D	F		F	D	F	
In	and	out,		'Round	a-	bout,	

F	D	F	D	F	D	F	
O	U	T	and	that	spells	out!	

What color are your bean bags?

Teacher's Edition

MUSIC STAFF AND TREBLE CLEF SIGN

TEACHER INSTRUCTIONS
Objects Needed
- Board or chart to draw music staff.
- Green and black markers.

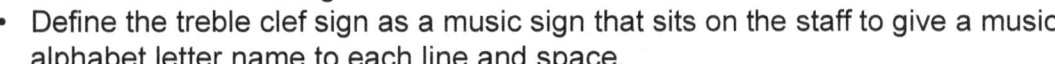

STAFF
Draw the first line in a thick black line and the second line in a thick green line.
The green line will be a helper for G line location on the treble clef staff.
Touch and count the 5 lines, starting at the bottom. Touch and count the 4 spaces, starting at the bottom. Students will count the lines and spaces with you.

Guide the students to identify these specific places as they touch and name the locations:

- Bottom black line is line 1.
- Green line is line 2.
- Space between the bottom black line and the green line is space 1.
- Space below the bottom black line is space under the staff.

TREBLE CLEF SIGN
- Draw the treble clef sign on the staff.
- Define the treble clef sign as a music sign that sits on the staff to give a music alphabet letter name to each line and space.
- Name space 1 as F and space under the staff as D as you draw the two notes. Guide the students to develop an understanding that the note head sits in the space. Add note stem and shade in the note head to make it a "ta" or quarter note.
- Students touch and name the notes on the music staff on student book page 22.
- Students will find F and D on the keyboard then play and sing the note names.

SONGS ON THE TREBLE CLEF
- Students discover familiar songs now written on the staff.
- Students touch and sing the note names of each song.
- Students play and sing the note names then the words.

Play and Play Piano Book for Beginners

MUSIC STAFF

The music staff is where the notes sit. The music staff is made up of lines and spaces.

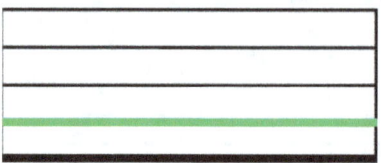

Find these places on the music staff:
- Touch the thick black bottom line with your pencil point. That is line 1.
- Touch the green line above it. That is line 2.
- Touch the space that is found between the bottom black line and the green line. That is space 1.
- Touch the space that is found below the bottom black line. That is called space under the staff.

TREBLE CLEF SIGN

The treble clef sign sits on the music staff. This sign gives each line and space a letter name from the music alphabet.

F is the name of space 1 on the staff. Touch **F** space note with your pencil point.

D is the name of the space under the staff. Touch **D** space note with your pencil point.

Play and sing the notes on the music staff below.

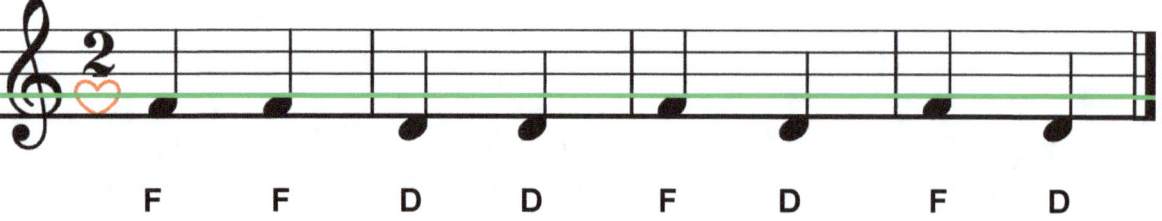

THREE SONGS USING F AND D

TEACHER INSTRUCTIONS
The songs, *"Rain, Rain"*, *"Doggie, Doggie"* and *"In and Out"* are re-introduced with F and D on the music staff. Sing the songs and play the game before students read and play the music on the piano/keyboard.

GAME DIRECTIONS
"Rain, Rain"
Sing the song and tap the heartbeat with fingertips on top of head to represent "raindrops" falling. Sing the song again, tapping the rhythm with fingertips on top of head.

"Doggie, Doggie"
See page 36 for story and game instructions.

"In and Out"
See page 12 for game instructions.

PIANO/KEYBOARD INSTRUCTIONS
Students will follow the instructions as given on their song sheets, pages 23-25.

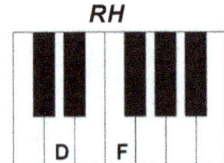

RAIN, RAIN

INSTRUCTIONS
Clap and read the rhythm.
Put finger 4 on F. Remember, F is found in the bottom space of the staff. D is found in the space under the staff.
Play and sing the note names then play and sing the words.

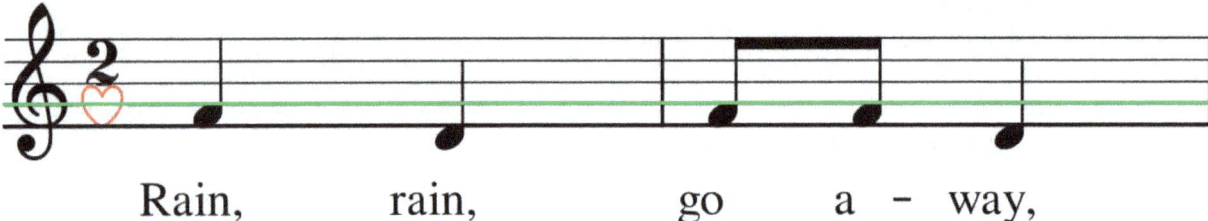

Come again some other day!

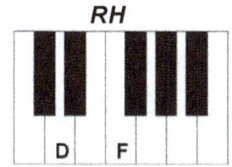

DOGGIE, DOGGIE

INSTRUCTIONS
Clap and read the rhythm.
Put finger 4 of your right hand on F.
Play and sing the note names then play and sing the words.

Dog - gie,   Dog - gie,   where's your   bone?

Someone stole it from your home!

Who   stole   my   bone?

Play and Play Piano Book for Beginners

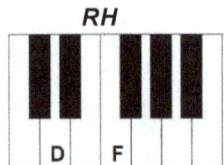

IN AND OUT

INSTRUCTIONS
Clap and read the rhythm.
Put finger 4 of your right hand on F. Finger 2 will play D.
Play and sing the note names, then play and sing the words.

In and out, 'Round a - bout, O U

T and that spells out!

What color are your bean bags?

TREBLE CLEF WRITING ACTIVITY

TEACHER INSTRUCTIONS

Copy the music staves below.

Students will:

- Trace the Treble Clef sign.
- Draw *F F D D* quarter notes on the first staff.
- Draw *F D F* quarter notes and a quarter rest on the second staff.
- Play the music they have written.

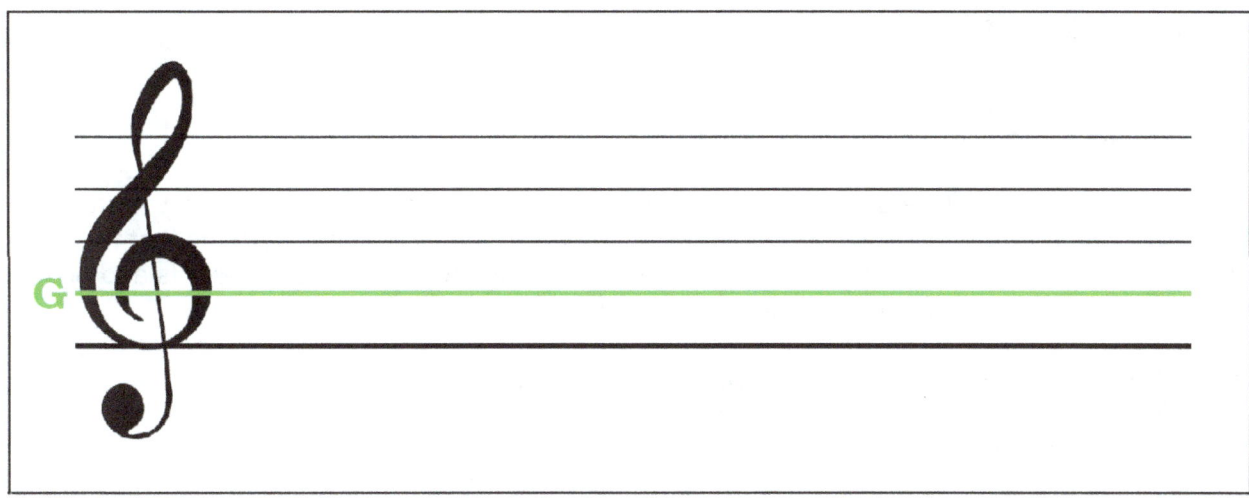

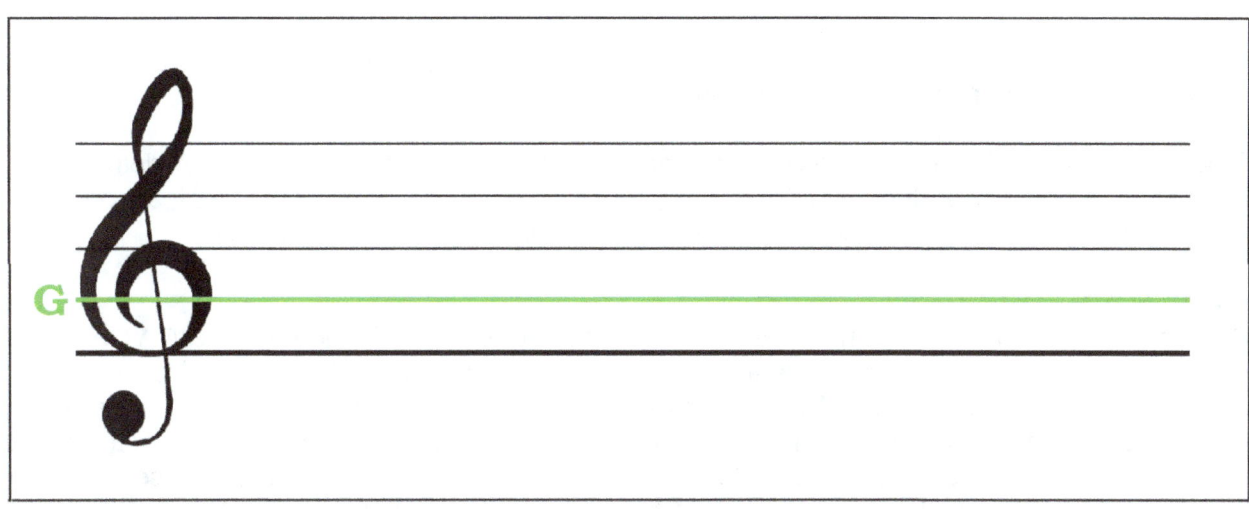

LEMONADE

TEACHER INSTRUCTIONS
Sing the song and play the game before students read and play the music on the piano/keyboard.

The music of the last phrase of the song is not on the student page because of the D to G skip that will be introduced later:

GAME DIRECTIONS
Object Needed

- Sign for the wall that says NEW YORK

This game is similar to *Charades*. Define the word *trade* as a job or work. Explain to the students that they must use only motions, not words or sounds to show a trade. Tell the students that this is a singing conversation. Sing the song for the children, pointing to self on the red words and pointing out in front on the blue words to indicate that others will be singing.

At the end of the song, pretend to be making lemonade with these motions:
- Hold drinking glass in one hand.
- Take half of lemon in the other hand and squeeze juice into glass.
- Take pitcher by the handle and pour water into the glass.
- Put in 2 spoons of sugar and stir.
- Put in a straw.
- Hold it out in front to indicate serving lemonade to someone.

Discuss the motions with the students and remind them that only motions were used. Sing again, the students do the lemonade motions with you.

Sing again and tell the students to watch for motions because you may trick them by doing the motions for a new trade. Suggestions for a different trade include: hairdresser, chef, school bus driver, store check-out person at the cash register. Students guess the new trade.

GAME FORMATION
Students form Team 1 by making a line straight across against a wall under the NEW YORK sign. Other students for Team 2 form a line against the opposite wall, facing Team 1. Guide Team 1 to secretly decide on a new trade. Team 1 begins the song, skipping toward Team 2 maintaining some distance apart from them as they sing the whole song. Team 2 sings the blue words. At the end of the song, Team 2 must guess Team 1's trade based upon their motions. If Team 2 guesses correctly, Team 1 must quickly get back to NEW YORK before Team 2 tags them. If any student is tagged, they become part of the other team. The game is played again as the children change sides and teams.

PIANO/KEYBOARD INSTRUCTIONS
Students will follow the instructions to the song as given in their student book.

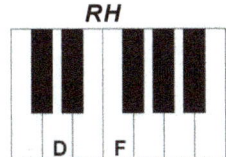

LEMONADE

INSTRUCTIONS
Clap and read the rhythm.
Put finger 4 of your right hand on F.
Play and sing the note names then play and sing the words.
This game song has two parts. It is a conversation. Take turns playing the different parts with your teacher or another student. One part is in red and the other part is in blue.

Here we come!   Where from?   New York.

What's your trade?   Lem-on-ade.   Give us some!   Have none!

Get to work and make us some!

Play and Play Piano Book for Beginners

DUCKS AND GEESE

TEACHER INSTRUCTIONS
Sing the song and play the game before students read and play the music on the piano/keyboard.*

GAME DIRECTIONS
Objects Needed
- Chair or other object for the "woods" where the wolf will be hiding
- Blue paper on the floor to represent water
- Piece of cloth or tissue for "kitty cat's tail"
- Boundary for "home"

This is a *"Call and Response"* game. The *"children"* are away from *"Mother"* in one area representing the woods. *"Wolf"* is hiding further in the woods. *"Mother"* is standing near the boundary representing home. *"Mother"* sings, the *"children"* answer. *"Mother's"* words are written in red and the *"children's"* words are written in blue. The *"wolf"* acts out the words of the song. At the end of the song, *"Mother"* claps, the *"children"* run to her, and the *"wolf"* tries to catch them before they reach home.

Students will sing but not play the last phrase of the song, "on the kitty cat's tail" as indicated by the words written at the bottom of their song sheet. The music for the last phrase is not notated in the student book because some of the notes are unknown to the students at this time.

PIANO/KEYBOARD INSTRUCTIONS
Students will follow the instructions as given on their song sheet.

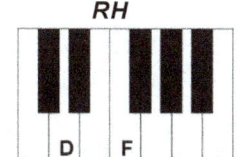

DUCKS AND GEESE

INSTRUCTIONS
Clap and read the rhythm.
Put finger 4 of your right hand on F.
Play and sing the note names then play and sing the words.
Play and sing the words that are in red while your teacher or another student plays and sings the words that are in blue.

Come home all my ducks and geese.　No we won't!

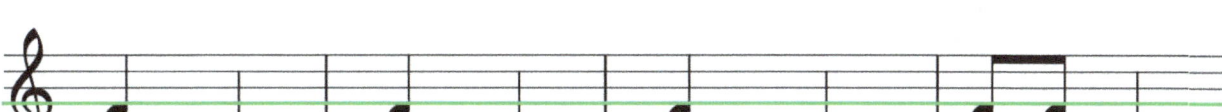

Why not?　'Cause not!　What's wrong?　It's the wolf!

Where's he hid-ing?　In the woods.　Do-ing what?　Wash-ing.

Where's he wash-ing?　By the lit-tle riv - er.　What's he dry his

hands　　on?

On the kitty cat's tail!

Play and Play Piano Book for Beginners

49

TWO SONGS INTRODUCING *G* LINE OF TREBLE CLEF
"BOUNCE HIGH" AND *"LUCY LOCKET"*

TEACHER INSTRUCTIONS
Sing the songs and play the game before students read and play the music on the piano/keyboard.

GAME DIRECTIONS
See page 16 for *"Bounce High"* and page 22 for *"Lucy Locket"* game directions.

PIANO/KEYBOARD INSTRUCTIONS
Objects Needed
- Music Staff on chart or whiteboard
- Green and Black Markers

Students will say the music alphabet.
Students identify the two notes they have read from the staff, *F* and *D*.
Students name *G* as the letter name after *F*.
Draw *F* and *G* on the music staff.

Guide the students to discover *G* is line 2 of the staff and that *G* is colored green to help identify it's name and location on the staff.
Students will draw *F* and *G* on the music staff.
Guide the students to discover that *G* is the next white key to the right of *F* on the keyboard.
Students will play the notes. Finger 4 will play *F* and finger 5 will play *G*.

Draw *D,F,G* on the music staff.

Students will draw *D,F,G* on the music staff then play and sing the note names.
Finger 2 will play *D*.

Draw the following 4 measure exercise on the board. The students will play and sing the note names.

Students will follow instructions as given in their student book for the songs.

BOUNCE HIGH

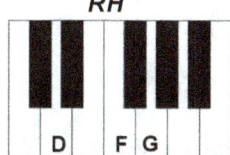

INSTRUCTIONS

Touch the notes and read the rhythm.
Clap and read the rhythm.
Put your right hand finger 4 on F. Finger 5 will play G.
Play and sing the note names.
Play and sing the words.

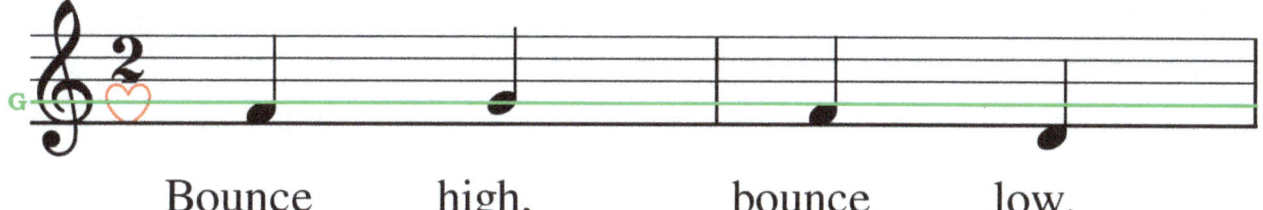

Bounce high, bounce low.

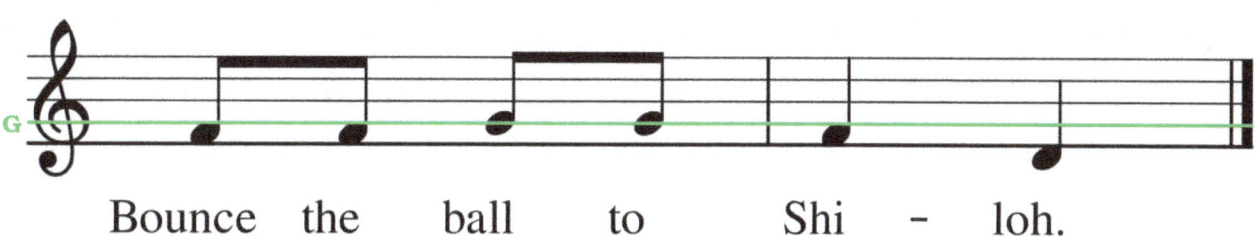

Bounce the ball to Shi - loh.

Play and Play Piano Book for Beginners

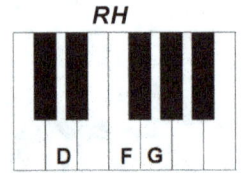

LUCY LOCKET

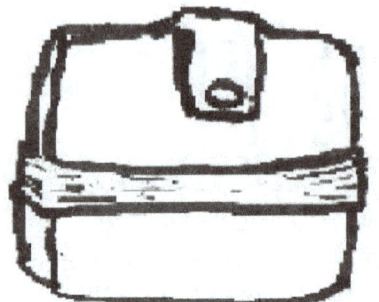

INSTRUCTIONS
Clap and read the rhythm.
Put your right hand finger 4 on F. Finger 5 will play G.
Play and sing the note names then play and sing the words.

Luc - y Loc - ket   lost her poc - ket,   Kit - ty Fish - er   found it.

Not a pen - ny   was there in it,   on - ly rib - bon 'round it.

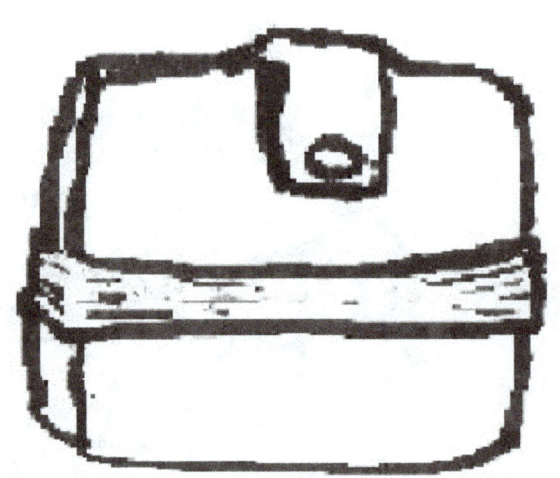

POSTCARD GAME

INSTRUCTIONS
Copy and cut the four patterns below to become postcards.
Give each student a set of the four cards. Students place all four cards in front of them.

STORY: *I need to mail some postcards. But before I mail them, I need you to help me check and see if I have every card. Please listen as I play and sing a pattern that is on a card. Hold up the card when you find it.*

Play and sing the note names to each card one at a time. The students hold up the correct card then sing it with you.

OTHER ACTIVITIES:

1. Student goes to a keyboard and places all four cards on the music rack. Student chooses one card to play and sing. The other students hold up the correct card.

2. Play each card without singing the note names. Students sing the note names then hold up the correct card.

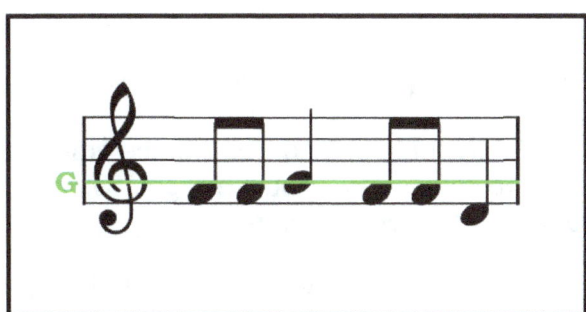

Play and Play Piano Book for Beginners

PLAINSIES, CLAPSIES

TEACHER INSTRUCTIONS
Sing the song and play the game before the students play the music on the piano/keyboard.

GAME DIRECTIONS
Object Needed
- Ball

The ball is not bounced but tossed, along with other hand motions listed below.

SONG WORDS	HAND MOTIONS
"Plainsies,	Toss ball up and catch it.
clapsies,	Toss ball up, clap hands, catch it.
Twirl around to backsies	Pass ball around back from one hand to other *Alternate motions:* Toss ball up, twirl hands around back while ball is in the air.
Right hand,	Hold ball out to side with right hand.
left hand,	Hold ball out to side with left hand.
Toss it high,	Toss ball high in air and catch it.
toss it low	Toss ball low in air and catch it.
Touch your knee, touch your toe, touch your heel	Toss the ball up, touch knee, catch ball; repeat toss and catch while touching toe then heel.
And through you go."	Move ball between legs in a figure eight motion.

PIANO/KEYBOARD INSTRUCTIONS

Guide students to discover that the first two lines of the song are the same as the previous song, "Bounce High". Students play F with their fourth finger and G with their fifth finger.

Have students take turns playing and singing the song on the piano/keyboard while others play the game.

Teacher's Edition

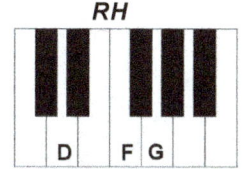

PLAINSIES, CLAPSIES

INSTRUCTIONS
Clap and read the rhythm.
Put your right hand finger 4 on F. Finger 5 will play G.
Play and sing the note names then play and sing the words.

Plain - sies,   clap - sies,   twirl a - round to   back - sies.

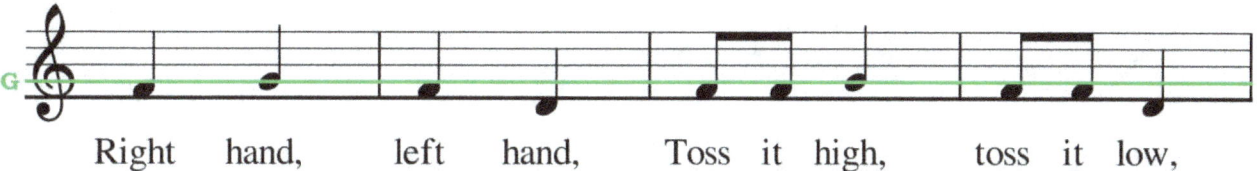

Right   hand,   left   hand,   Toss it high,   toss it low,

touch your knee,   touch your toe.   Touch your heel and

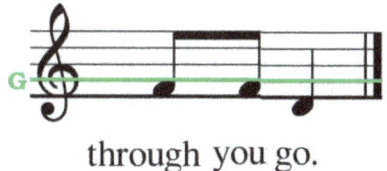

through you go.

Play and Play Piano Book for Beginners

WE ARE DANCING IN THE FOREST

TEACHER INSTRUCTIONS
Sing the song and play the game before the students play the music on the piano/keyboard.

GAME DIRECTIONS
Objects Needed
- Wolf mask, wolf hand puppet or picture of wolf for child to hold in front of face
- Chair for the "forest" and chair for "home"
- Copy of TE p. 58 for each student

One student is chosen to be the wolf and hides behind a chair, pretending to be in the forest. The other students sing the song, standing in between the wolf and home, dancing and moving as they sing. At the end of the song the students ask with their speaking voice, *"Oh wolf, are you there?"* The wolf can give silly answers such as *"No, I'm getting a pedicure"*; *"No, I had to go to the dentist"*; *"No, I had to fix a flat on my bike"*, etc. If the wolf's answer is no, the song begins again. If the wolf's answer is yes, the students run and tag the back of the other chair that is "home" and safe from the wolf.

PIANO/KEYBOARD INSTRUCTIONS
Students touch and sing the note names of the song. Students compare and contrast the music in *"We Are Dancing In the Forest"* to the music in the song, *"Lucy Locket"*. Guide students to discover the same music on lines 1 and 3 and the difference in beat 3 on lines 2 and 4.

The students play and sing the note names. The students play and sing the song. Students will draw a picture on page 58 and color their page 31 as they await their individual turn to play the song.

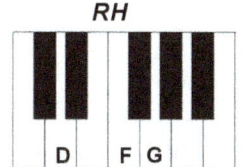

WE ARE DANCING IN THE FOREST

INSTRUCTIONS
Clap and read the rhythm.
Put finger 4 of your right hand on F. Finger 5 will play G.
Play and sing the note names then play and sing the words.

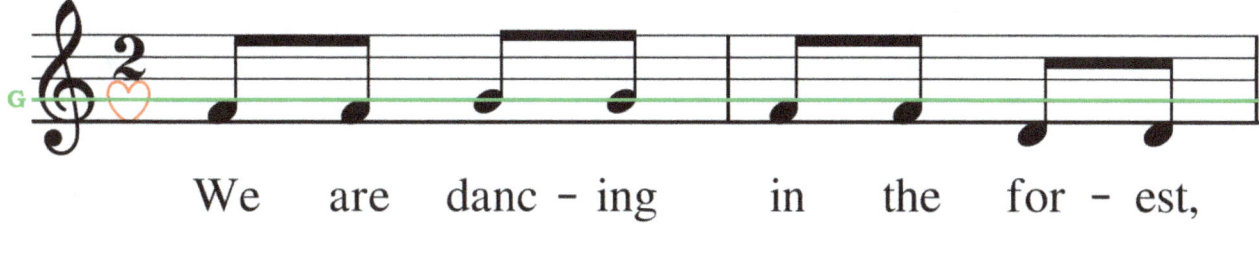

We are danc - ing in the for - est,

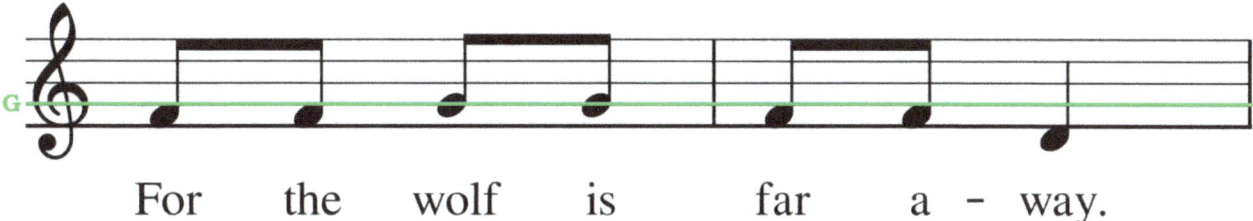

For the wolf is far a - way.

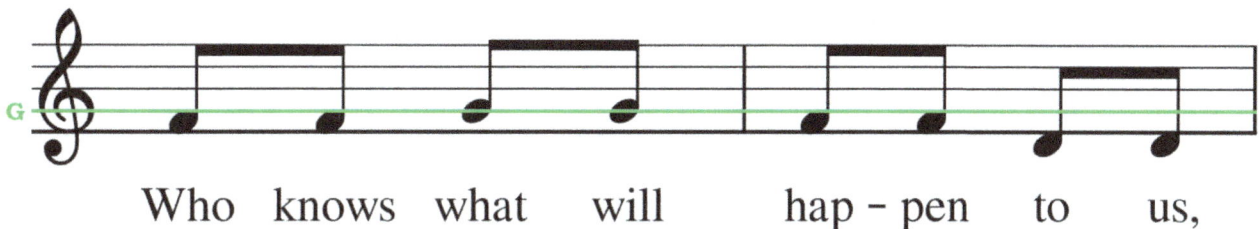

Who knows what will hap - pen to us,

If he finds us at our play?

(Spoken) *"Oh Wolf, are you there?"*

Play and Play Piano Book for Beginners

**Draw a picture of the forest.
Draw the children dancing in the forest.**

Color the picture of the wolf.

NANNY GOAT

TEACHER INSTRUCTIONS
Sing the song and play the game before students read and play the music on the piano/keyboard.

GAME DIRECTIONS
Objects Needed
- Two chairs with space in between to represent a stall in the barn.
- Copy of Staff paper, page 117.
- Green pencil color
- Pencil

Story: *The nanny goats were turned out of their stalls early in the morning. They went far out into the pasture to run and play. The billy goats were left in the barn. Later, the billy goats were turned out of their stalls. They ran out to the pasture. When they saw the nanny goats already playing, they decided to tease them. They were brave and got very close to the nanny goats. The nanny goats heard them and tried to catch them. The billy goats were not very brave because when the nanny goats began to chase them, they turned and ran to safety back into their stall.*

Game: "Nanny Goat" is far away from the "Billy Goat" in the stall. "Billy Goat" leaves the stall, gets close to "Nanny Goat" and sings the song. Teacher claps at the end of the song to signal "Nanny Goat" to catch "Billy Goat". "Billy Goat" is safe if he gets back to the stall before "Nanny Goat" tags him.

PIANO/KEYBOARD INSTRUCTIONS
This song introduces the D-G interval, which is called a "jump."
On your copy of the staff paper, draw a Treble Clef sign, trace the *G* second line with a green pencil color, and write *G* beside the second line. Guide students to do the same. Draw exercise 1 on the staff as shown below. Guide the students to develop an understanding that the G line note jumps over the *F* space. Students will draw exercise one. Draw exercises two and three. Students will do the same. Students will play and sing these exercises.

1. 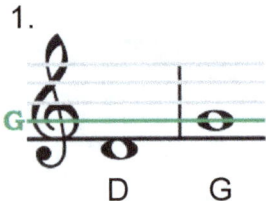 2.  3.

Students will follow instructions as given on page 33 in their student book.

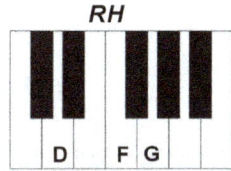

NANNY GOAT

INSTRUCTIONS
Clap and read the rhythm.
Put finger 4 of your right hand on F.
Play and sing the note names. Watch for the jump from D to G.
Play and sing the words.

Nan - ny,   Nan - ny   Nan - ny   Goat,

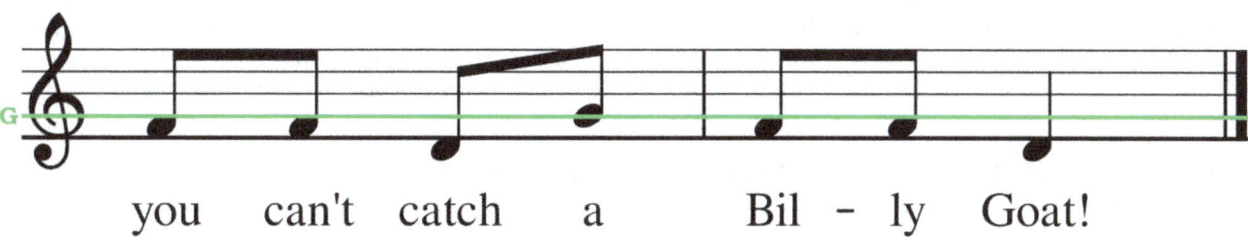

you   can't   catch   a   Bil - ly   Goat!

Play and Play Piano Book for Beginners

JOHNNY'S IT

TEACHER INSTRUCTIONS Sing the song and play the game before the students read and play the music on the piano/keyboard.

GAME DIRECTIONS

Objects Needed

- 2 chairs
- blindfold

Story: *Johnny was a boy in school just about your age. He was very smart but he had trouble paying attention in class. He was easily distracted. His teacher saw that he was busy looking around the room and not doing his arithmetic problems. Arithmetic is a word that means math. She told Johnny, "Johnny, you move to the empty chair at the front of the row. Do not turn around! Get your arithmetic problems done now!" Johnny moved to the front of the row and started trying to solve his arithmetic problems. He became frustrated because he had not listened to the teacher earlier when she had explained how to do the math problems and now he found the work hard to do. Then, another thing caused him to become even more frustrated! Someone right behind him whispered to him, "Hello, who am I?" Johnny knew he could not turn around. He knew the teacher meant business! He sat there, trying to think of who was whispering to him. He had trouble recognizing the voice and that made him even more frustrated.*

Two chairs are lined up, one behind the other. One student, "Johnny", sits in the front chair, eyes closed and blindfolded. Another student sits behind in the second chair. Students sing the first two phrases of the song. The student behind Johnny sings alone, *"Hello, who am I?"* Johnny tries to guess who is in the chair behind him.

PIANO/KEYBOARD INSTRUCTIONS

Have the students circle the D-G skip in the music. Students will follow the instructions as given in their student book.

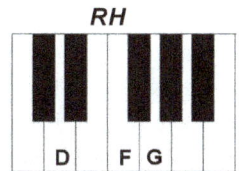

JOHNNY'S IT

INSTRUCTIONS
Clap and read the rhythm.
Put your right hand finger 4 on F. Watch for the jump from D to G.
Play and sing the note names then play and sing the words.

John - ny's it, he had a fit. He can't do a -

rith - me - tic. "Hel - lo, who am I?"

Play and Play Piano Book for Beginners

INTRODUCING TREBLE CLEF FIRST LINE *E*
"LEMONADE"

TEACHER INSTRUCTIONS
Sing the song and play the game before the students read and play the music on the piano/keyboard.

GAME DIRECTIONS
See page 46 for "*Lemonade*" game directions.

PIANO/KEYBOARD INSTRUCTIONS
Objects Needed:
- Copy of Staff paper, page 117.
- Green pencil color
- Pencil

This song introduces first line *E* of the treble clef. Write the music alphabet on the board and underline *D E F:* A B C <u>D E F</u> G. Guide the students to develop an understanding that *E* is the note between *D* and *F*.

On your copy of the staff paper, draw a Treble Clef sign, trace the G second line with a green pencil color, and write *G* beside the second line. Guide students to do the same. Draw exercise one on the staff as shown below. Guide the students to develop an understanding that *E* is located on line one. Identify *E* as a step up from *D* space and that *F* is a step up from *E* line. Students will draw exercise one. Draw exercises two and three. Students will do the same. Students will play and sing these exercises.

Students will follow the instructions to the song as given in their student book.

1.

2.

3.

64 Teacher's Edition

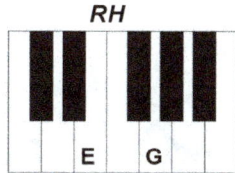

LEMONADE

INSTRUCTIONS
Here is an old game song It is found in a new place on the staff.
Put finger 5 of your right hand on G. Finger 3 will play E.
Play and sing the note names, then play and sing the words.
Play the different parts as you did before.

Here we come!   Where from?   New York.

What's your trade?   Lem-on-ade.   Give us some!   Have none!

Get to work and make us some!

Play and Play Piano Book for Beginners

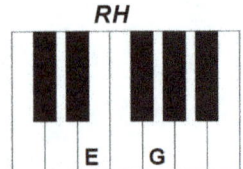

IN AND OUT

INSTRUCTIONS
Here is an old game song. It is found in a new place on the staff.
Put finger 5 of your right hand on G. Finger 3 will play E.
Play and sing the note names then play and sing the words.

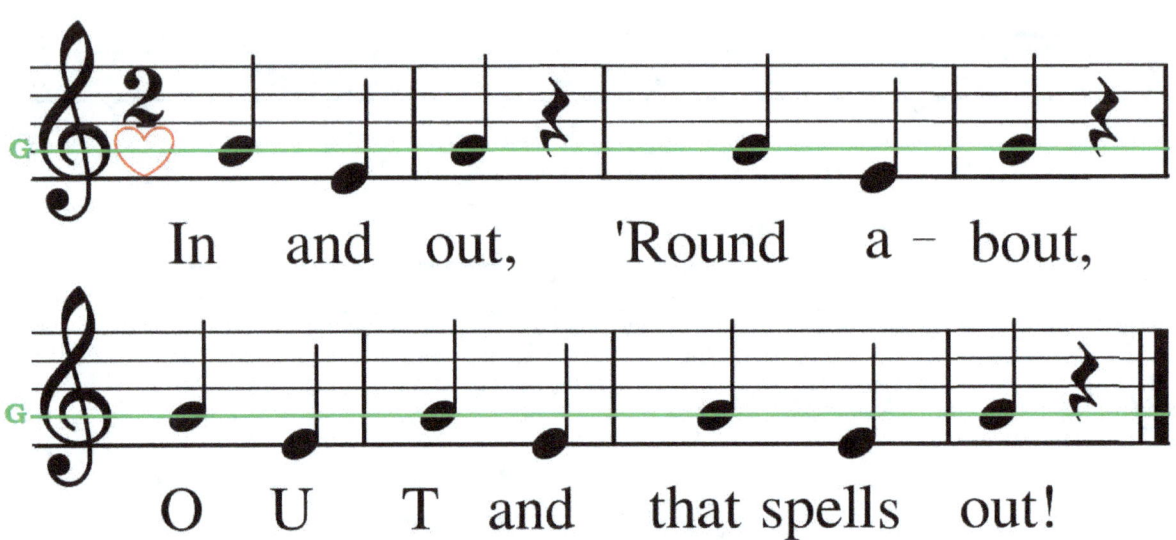

In and out, 'Round a - bout,

O U T and that spells out!

What color are
your bean bags?

Teacher's Edition

TREBLE CLEF A

PIANO/KEYBOARD INSTRUCTIONS

Write the music alphabet twice on the board. **A B C D E F G A B C D E F G**

Draw Figures 1 and 2 on the treble clef staff as shown below.

1.    2.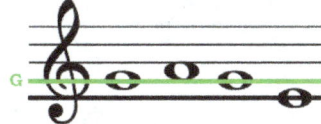

Guide the students to develop an understanding that:

- The next note name after *G* in the music alphabet is *A*.
- *A* is found in space 2 on the Treble clef staff.
- *A* is a step above *G* and is found between the second and third black keys of the 3 black key group.

Play and sing the note names then have the students play and sing.

Students will follow instructions as given in their student book.

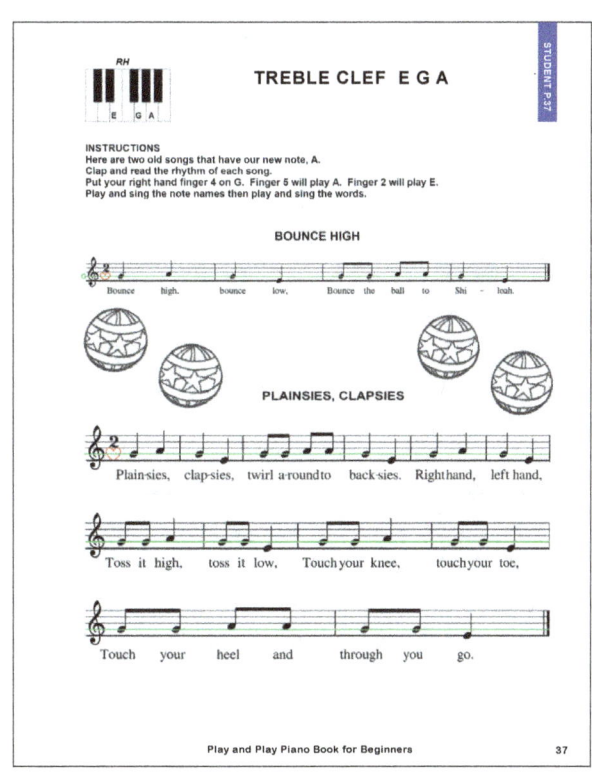

Play and Play Piano Book for Beginners

TREBLE CLEF F G A

PIANO/KEYBOARD INSTRUCTIONS

Draw Figures 1 and 2 on the treble clef staff as shown below.

1.    2.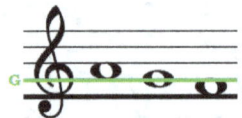

Guide the students to identify that *F G A* are touching three black key group.

Students will follow instructions for the song, FROG IN THE MEADOW as given in their student book, page 38.

HOP OLD SQUIRREL

TEACHER INSTRUCTIONS
Sing the song and play the game before students read and play the music on the piano/keyboard.

GAME DIRECTIONS
Story: *The young squirrels were supposed to be gathering nuts to store up for winter. But, just like children your age, the squirrels wanted to play instead of doing their chores. They were feeling frisky in the nice fall weather. The squirrels were playing a hopping game.*

Students scatter throughout the room. They must hop on one foot around the room throughout the song. The other foot must not touch the floor but should be moving "fancy", any way the students choose. Remind students that they should not just hop in place but must hop around the room as they move the other foot at the same time. If the other foot touches the floor, the student must sit.

MUSIC INSTRUCTIONS
Students will follow the instructions to the song as given in their student book.

Play and Play Piano Book for Beginners

MIDDLE C POSITION

TEACHER INSTRUCTIONS
Write the music alphabet on the board. Students will read the music alphabet forward and backward.

A B <u>C</u> D <u>E</u> F G

Draw a line under the *C D E* letter names, <u>C</u> <u>D</u> <u>E</u>. Have the students say these three note names forward and backward.

Draw *E D C* on the music staff, as shown in exercise 1 as illustrated below. Students will review *D* and *E* locations on the staff. Name the new note as *Middle C*. Guide the students to develop an understanding that *Middle C* has a ledger line through the middle of the note. The ledger line gives *Middle C* its line place under the staff, which is a step down from *D*.
Students will draw and play the notes in exercise 1.

Draw the notes in exercises 2 and 3. The students will read and play the notes.

PIANO/KEYBOARD INSTRUCTIONS
Students will play *Middle C D E* in the songs, *Hot Cross Buns, Frog in the Meadow* (page 32 for game instructions*), Hop Old Squirrel* (page 72 for game instructions), and *Closet Key* (page 30 for game instructions). Students will follow the instructions for each song as given in their student book.

HOT CROSS BUNS

INSTRUCTIONS
Clap and read the rhythm.
Put your right hand thumb on Middle C.
Finger 2 will play D. Finger 3 will play E.
Play and sing the note names then play and sing the words.

Hot cross buns, Hot cross buns, One a pen-ny,

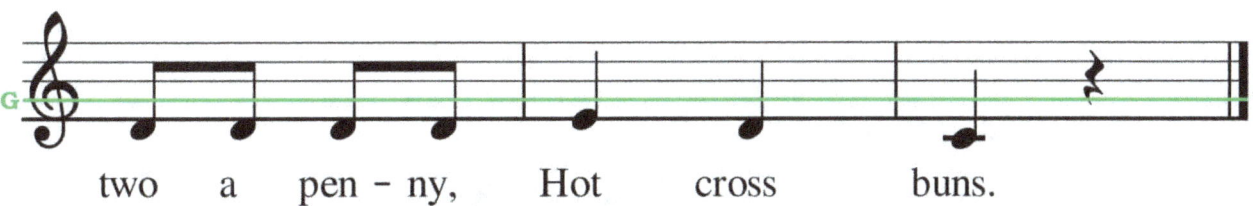

two a pen - ny, Hot cross buns.

Play and Play Piano Book for Beginners

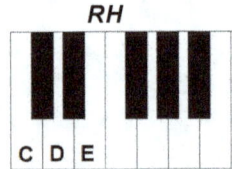

FROG IN THE MEADOW

INSTRUCTIONS
Clap and read the rhythm.
Put your right hand thumb on Middle C.
Finger 2 will play D. Finger 3 will play E.
Play and sing the note names then play and sing the words.

Frog   in the   mea-dow,   can't get him   out.   Take a lit-tle

stick   and   stir   him   a - bout.

Leap, leap, leap, down!

72   Teacher's Edition

HOP OLD SQUIRREL

INSTRUCTIONS
Clap and read the rhythm.
Put your right hand thumb on Middle C.
Finger 2 will play D. Finger 3 will play E.
Play and sing the note names then play and sing the words.

Hop old squirrel, ei – dl-dum, ei – dl-dum, Hop old

squirrel, ei-dl-dum dee; Hop old squirrel, ei – dl-dum,

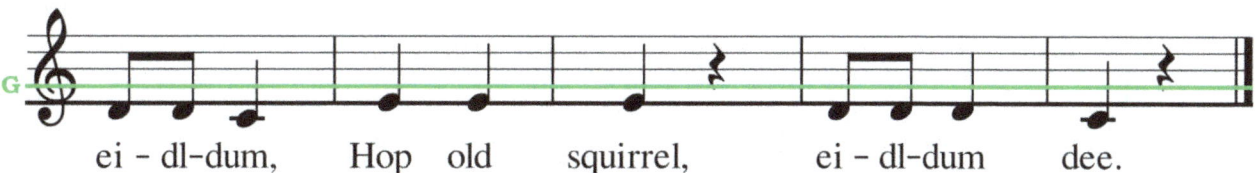

ei – dl-dum, Hop old squirrel, ei – dl-dum dee.

Play and Play Piano Book for Beginners

CLOSET KEY

INSTRUCTIONS
Clap and read the rhythm.
Put your right hand thumb on Middle C.
Finger 2 will play D. Finger 3 will play E.
Play and sing the note names then play and sing the words.

I have lost the clos-et key, in that lad-y's gar - den.

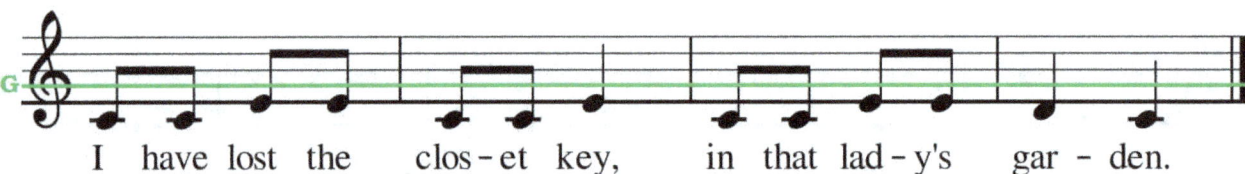

I have lost the clos-et key, in that lad-y's gar - den.

TREBLE CLEF NOTE NAME MATCH

INSTRUCTIONS

Copy the worksheet below for each student.

Students draw a line to match the music alphabet name to the correct note on the staff.

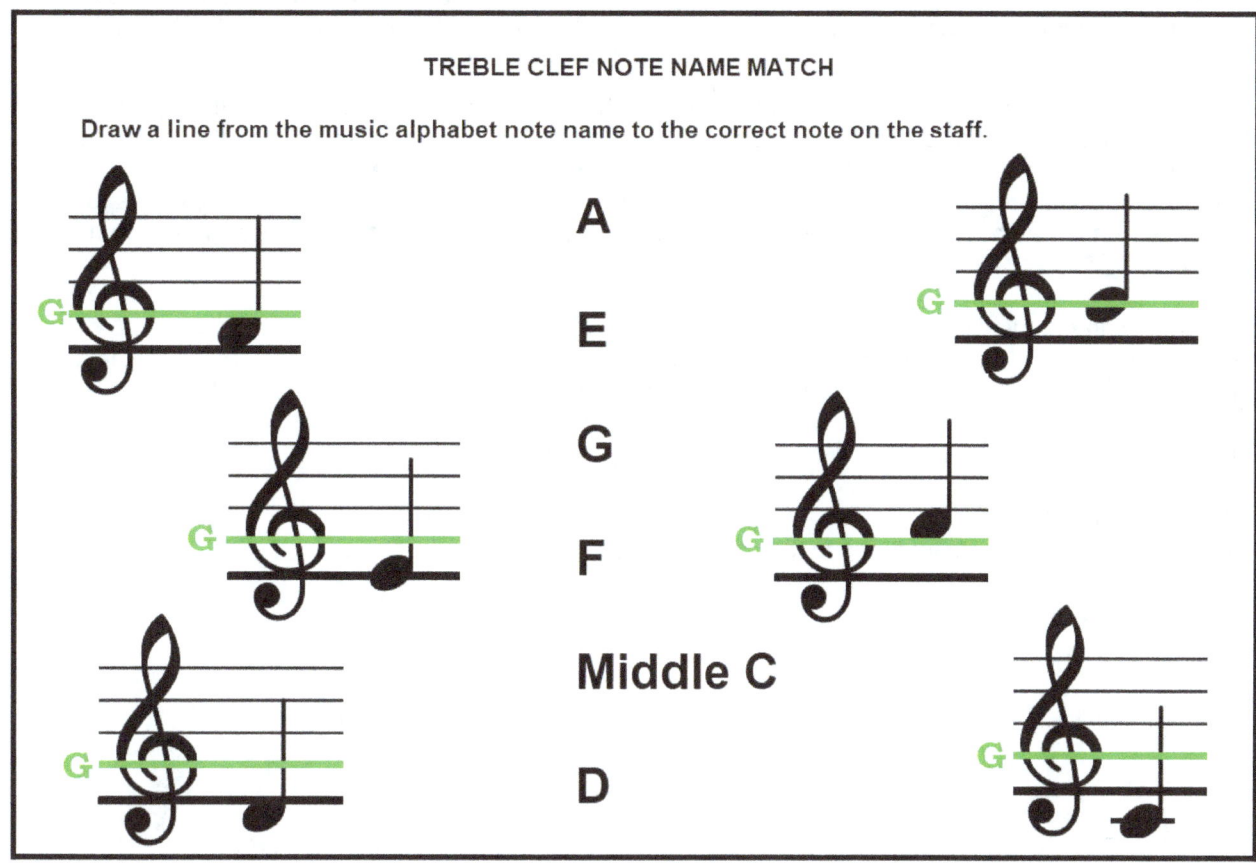

BUTTON, YOU MUST WANDER

TEACHER INSTRUCTIONS
Sing the song and play the game before introducing the song in the student book.

GAME INSTRUCTIONS
Objects Needed
- Large button or large bead. The hole in the button or bead or button should be large enough for the knot of the string to easily pass through it.
- Cotton string. The string should be long enough for all the students to be able to hold it with both hands when the ends are tied to make a circle. Thread the string through the hole in the button or bead. Tie the ends securely then re-inforce the knot with clear glue.

Students stand in a circle and hold the string with both hands. One of the students has the "button" covered in one hand. One student is in the middle of the circle with eyes closed. The other students sing the song, passing the button around the circle as they sing. The students should keep the "button" covered as they pass it around the string to the person next to them. Guide the students to move their hands to the beat of the song and pretend to be passing the button even when they do not have it.

The student in the middle opens his/her eyes at measure 9 when the words, *"bright eyes will find you…"* are sung. Students holding the string continue to pass the "button". The challenge is to keep it hidden as it is passed because the child in the middle is now watching. Students holding the string keep their hands still at the end of the song. One child will have the 'button" and the child in the middle guesses who has it.

MUSIC INSTRUCTIONS
Students will follow the instructions to the song as given in their student book.

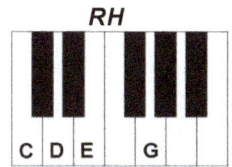

BUTTON, YOU MUST WANDER

INSTRUCTIONS
Clap and read the rhythm.
Put your right hand thumb on Middle C.
Play and sing the note names then play and sing the words.

But-ton, you must wan-der, wan-der, wan-der, But-ton, you must

wan-der, ev-'ry-where. Bright eyes will find you, Sharp eyes will

find you, But-ton, you must wan-der ev-'ry-where!

Play and Play Piano Book for Beginners

DADDY SHOT A BEAR

TEACHER INSTRUCTIONS
Sing the song and play the game before introducing the song in the student book.

GAME INSTRUCTIONS
Objects Needed
- Picture of Bear
- Water Spray Bottle labeled "BEAR SPRAY SECRET FORMULA: H20"
- Water in the spray bottle
- Picture of log cabin door with cut-out at the keyhole

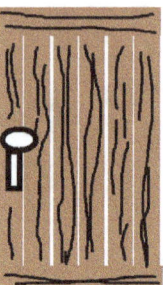

Story: Daddy and family lived in a log cabin. The door and the windows did not have glass, just solid wood. Daddy and family loved to sing and dance. Bear watched them through the open window and saw how much fun they were having. He especially liked the way they kept the steady beat in their feet. He wanted to join the fun. He went up to the front porch of the cabin and joined in the song, keeping the steady beat just like them. (Sing the song, step the steady beat, touch the floor on the last beat of the song.) Daddy saw the bear. He did not know it was a friendly bear! He quickly closed the door and the wooden shutters of the windows. He got out the bear spray. He could only aim the bear spray bottle through the keyhole opening. The bear would not stay still! He marched around the porch and touched the floor on the last beat of the song. That is when Daddy tried to spray him with the bear spray. Daddy missed! He sprayed right when the bear ducked down to touch the floor. Daddy could not see through the keyhole. The bear thought this was great fun and stood up to march and sing again.

Game: "Bear" holds the bear picture in front of his/her face. "Daddy" stands away from the bear, but within range with the spray bottle. The nozzle of the spray bottle is in the keyhole opening of the log cabin door picture. All sing the song while "bear" keeps steady beat in feet, then touches the floor on the last beat of the song. "Daddy" sprays water on the last beat and tries to spray the "bear" before the "bear" touches the floor.

MUSIC INSTRUCTIONS
Guide the students to develop an understanding that familiar notes, *F* and *G*, have been added to the *Middle C D E* pattern in this new song.

Students will follow the instructions to the song as given in their student book.

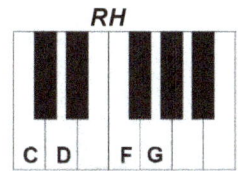

DADDY SHOT A BEAR

INSTRUCTIONS
Clap and read the rhythm.
Put your right hand thumb on Middle C.
Play and sing the name names then play and sing the words.

Dad-dy shot a bear,   Dad-dy shot a bear,

Shot him through the key-hole, and nev-er touched a hair!

Play and Play Piano Book for Beginners

KING'S LAND

TEACHER INSTRUCTIONS
Sing the song and play the game before introducing the song in the student book.

GAME INSTRUCTIONS
Objects Needed
- Crown
- Poster or large picture showing "Combs for Sale"
- Designated boundary for "king's land" and "subjects' land"

Story: *When the king ruled, he gave his "subjects a small amount of land. The king had a large amount of land and did not allow his subjects on it. One day they learned the king was in Boston, shopping for combs for the queen. They decided to go on his land. While the king's subjects were having a good time on the land, the king started back home. The subjects were warned that the king was on his way. They hurried back across the boundary to their land before the king could capture them.*

Game: King wears the crown, with his back to the other students, shopping for combs. Students sing the song, arms linked together at elbows or arms across shoulders. They march the steady beat onto the king's land as they sing. At the end of the song, the teacher claps and the king turns around. The students let go of each other and run back across the boundary to their land. The king chases them and if he tags anyone, the captured student must go to Boston with the king, The captured subject must then help the king capture the others as the song is sung again.

Alternate movement: the students may move freely without touching each other, then run off the king's land to their side of the boundary at the end of the song.

PIANO/KEYBOARD INSTRUCTIONS
Have the students circle second space A 's in the song.
Students will follow the instructions to the song as given in their student book.

KING'S LAND

INSTRUCTIONS
Clap and read the rhythm.
Put your right hand thumb on Middle C.
Finger 5 will play G and A.
Play and sing the note names then play and sing the words.

I'm   on the   King's   land, the   King is not at   home.

He's   gone to   Bos - ton to   buy his wife a   comb.

NAUGHTY KITTY CAT

TEACHER INSTRUCTIONS
Sing the song and play the game before the students read and play the music on the piano/keyboard.

GAME DIRECTIONS
Object Needed

- Chair for "mouse hole" base

Students stand in random places throughout the room. One student is the mouse, who hides his/her eyes while another student is secretly chosen to be the cat. When the song begins, the mouse opens eyes and begins to move around the room, weaving around the other students. On the word, "*Scat!*", the cat chases the mouse. The mouse tries to reach the mouse hole, which means touch the back of the chair before being tagged by the cat.

PIANO/KEYBOARD INSTRUCTIONS

Students will follow the instructions to the song as given in their student book.

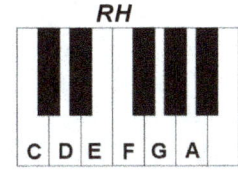

NAUGHTY KITTY CAT

INSTRUCTIONS
Clap and read the rhythm.
Put your right hand thumb on Middle C.
Finger 5 will play G and A.
Play and sing the note names then play and sing the words.

Naugh-ty kit-ty cat, you are ver-y fat! You have but-ter

on your whisk-ers, naugh-ty kit-ty cat! *Scat!*

RING AROUND THE ROSIE

TEACHER INSTRUCTIONS
Sing the song and play the game before students read and play the music on the piano/keyboard.

GAME DIRECTIONS
Objects needed

- Artificial rose
- White board or large chart for writing the four **S** words below.

Instruct the students to read and remember the four **S's** to the game.
Steady Beat
Slowly
Softly
Silly

Place rose in the center of the room. Student walks around the rose in a circle keeping a steady beat in feet. On the word *"down"*, student falls to the floor, remembering to fall slowly, softly, and any silly way he/she chooses. Encourage the students to make up original ways to fall down.

PIANO/KEYBOARD
Students will follow the instructions to the song as given in their student book.

RING AROUND THE ROSIE

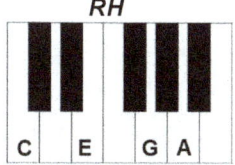

INSTRUCTIONS
Clap and read the rhythm.
Put your right hand thumb on Middle C.
Finger 5 will play G and A.
Play and sing the note names then play and sing the words.

Ring a-round the   ros - ie,   Poc-ket full of

pos-ies.   Ash-es,   ash-es,   all fall down!

Play and Play Piano Book for Beginners

WHO'S THAT TAPPING AT THE WINDOW

NEW RHYTHM: HALF NOTE

TEACHER INSTRUCTIONS Sing the song and play the game before the students read and play the music on the piano/keyboard.

GAME DIRECTIONS
Objects Needed
- Chair
- Blindfold
- Poster or picture on board of house with window and door 𝅗𝅥

Story: *Mother has to go next door. She tells her child, "I will just be gone 10 minutes. You are old enough to stay by yourself for that long. Just sit and watch t.v. Remember the rules: Do not let any stranger in!" The child watches t.v. for a couple of minutes then goes to sleep. Suddenly tapping and knocking is heard. The child knows not to open the door, but tries to figure out if the person at the door is a friend.*

Student sits in chair with blindfold on and sings verse one. Another student taps and knocks while singing verse two. Remind the student to tap and knock the way the words go in the song. Student in chair guesses who is tapping and knocking.

HALF NOTE INSTRUCTIONS
Sing the song and clap the rhythm, holding hands together when the word with the half notes are sung. Ask: *What are the words of the song that have the longer sound to hold?* (*"Who's that"* and *"I am"*)
Step the steady beat while singing the song and clapping the rhythm.
Ask: *How many times do you step when singing the longer sounds?*
Put two heartbeats on the board. Touch the two heartbeats each time the long word(s) are sung and clapped in the song. ♡ ♡

Put tie symbol, _____ , to connect the two heartbeats. Demonstrate that holding hands together for the long sound is shown by the tie, or curved line that joins the beats together.   ♡ ♡

Tie two ta's.

Demonstrate that two ta's tied together equal two heartbeats.

Change the tied notes to a half note. Name the new note as "ta-a". Instruct the students that the half note, with the note head not shaded in, is read as "ta-a" and equals two heartbeats.

𝅗𝅥 = ♡ ♡

Students will draw half notes on the board.

PIANO/KEYBOARD INSTRUCTIONS
Students will follow the instructions to the song as given in their student book.

WHO'S THAT TAPPING AT THE WINDOW?

INSTRUCTIONS
Circle the repeat sign.
Circle the half note.
Clap and read the rhythm. Remember to follow the repeat sign.
Put your right hand thumb on Middle C.
Play and sing the rhythm names then play and sing the words.

Who's   that   tap-ping at the   win-dow?   Who's   that
I   am   tap-ping at the   win-dow,   I   am

knock-ing at the door?
knock-ing at the door.

Play and Play Piano Book for Beginners

FRÈRE JACQUES

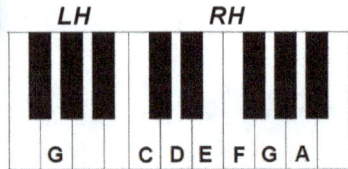

INSTRUCTIONS
Put two dots beside the double bar line to make it a repeat sign.
Clap and read the rhythm.
Put your right hand thumb on Middle C.
Finger 5 will play G and A.
Use your left hand finger 4 to play G that is written below the staff.
It is the G that is lower, or to the left of Middle C.
Play and sing the note names then play and sing the words.
Play and sing the song in a round with your teacher or another student.

Frè-re   Jac-ques,   Frè-re   Jac-ques,   Dor-mez   vous?

Dor-mez   vous?   Sonnez les ma-tin-es,   Sonnez les ma-tin-es,

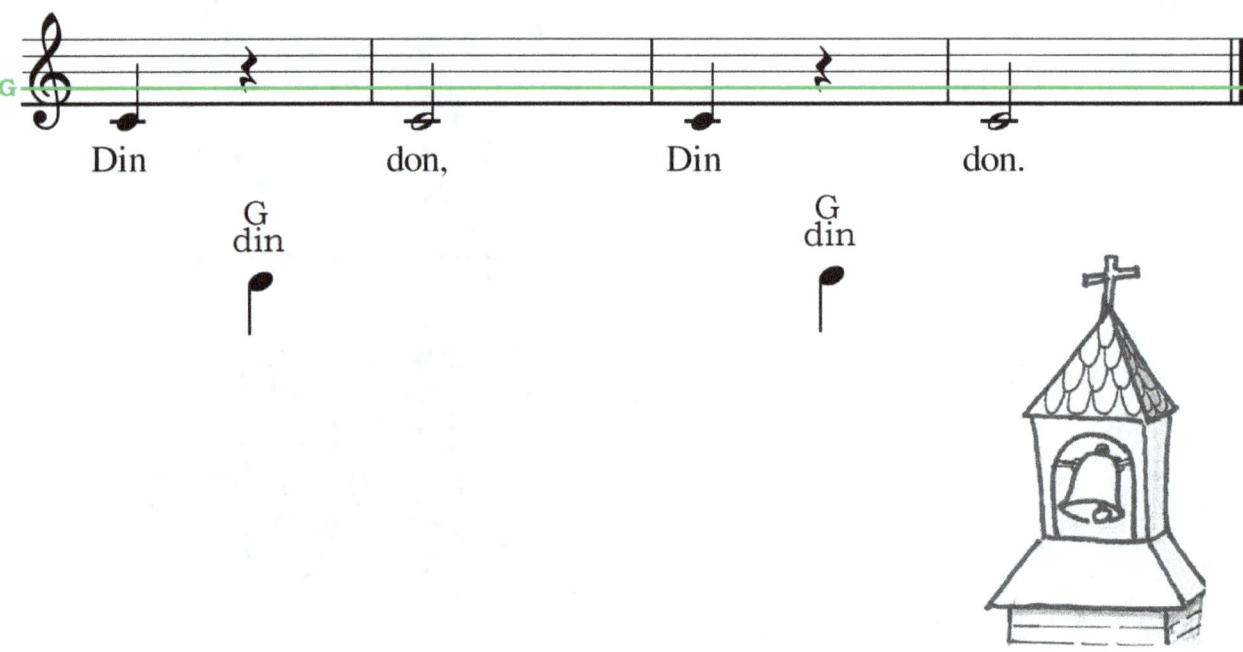

Din   don,   Din   don.

G din   G din

Teacher's Edition

OLD WOMAN
NEW NOTE - F#

TEACHER INSTRUCTIONS Sing the song and play the game before the students read and play the music on the piano/keyboard.

GAME DIRECTIONS

Objects Needed

- **2 chairs**
- **Hand drum**
- **Blue paper**
- **Green paper**
- **Piano**
- Story: *A young man's neighbor was an old woman. She said she was very hard of hearing and just sat in her house. The young man thought she might not be so hard of hearing. He thought maybe she didn't want to hear if there was any work to be done. One day he decided to give her a test. First he asked, "Old woman, old woman, are you fond of smoking?" This meant did she like to do the hard work of smoking or curing the meat. The old woman answered, "speak a little louder sir, I'm very hard of hearing!" (Sing verse 1.) He decided to ask a different question: "Old woman, old woman, are you fond of carding?" Carding was a hard chore. The job was to comb out the wool after the sheep had been sheared. (Sing verse 2.) He still thought she was not so hard of hearing and just didn't want to hear of work. He decided to ask a different question: "Old woman, old woman, don't you want me to court you?" To court someone is a old-fashioned word that means to get to know someone and decide if you want to marry. (Sing verse 3.) The young man said, "Just like I thought, she only hears what she wants to hear! I will give her one more test. He asked her: "Old woman, old woman, don't you want to marry me?" (Sing verse 4.) Oh, no! The old woman got up from her chair and started chasing the young man. He had to get away from the old woman. But, he had some obstacles to go through before he could get to his house. He had to jump over a large rock, jump over a small stream, go through some bushes, and run over some gravel that made lots of noise when he ran. Luckily, he made it home before the old woman caught him because she was slower as she followed him, running through the same obstacles.*

Play and Play Piano Book for Beginners

Old Woman, continued

Game: Place the props around the room to represent the obstacles: Hand drum represents the large rock; blue paper represents the stream; green paper represents the bushes; piano represents the gravel. The "Old woman" sits in one chair. The "young man" stands beside the other chair. At the end of the verse, the young man begins running, going through the "obstacles": hitting drum (large rock); jumping over the blue paper on the floor (stream); putting both hands on the green paper (bushes); playing the piano/keyboard with both hands, random playing anywhere on the keys (gravel); touching the back of his chair for home. The old woman starts after the young man and must go through the same obstacles as she tries to tag the young man. The young man is safe when he gets back to his chair.

PIANO/KEYBOARD INSTRUCTIONS

F-sharp, F♯, is introduced in this song. Demonstrate the F♯ location for the students. It is the black key which is to the right and touching white key F Guide the students to develop an understanding that a sharp sign ♯, in music means to go up one half step which means to the next key to the right on the keyboard.

Students will find F♯'s on the piano/keyboard.

Students will follow the instructions to the song as given in their student book.

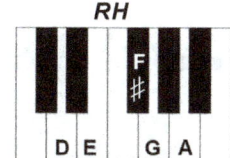

OLD WOMAN

INSTRUCTIONS
Circle all the F#'s in the song.
Clap and read the rhythm.
Put your right hand thumb on D. Finger 3 will play F#.
Play and sing the note names then play and sing the words.

1. Old wo-man, Old wo-man, are you fond of smok-ing?

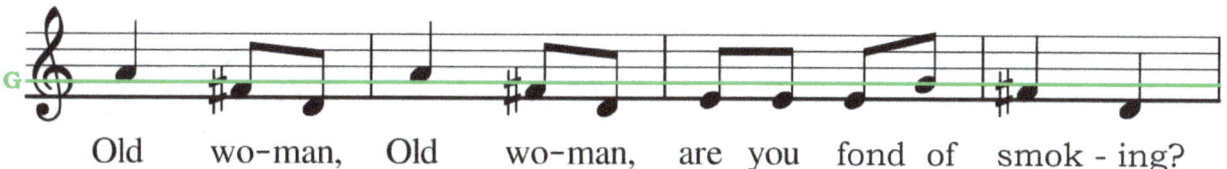
Old wo-man, Old wo-man, are you fond of smok-ing?

Speak a lit-tle loud-er sir, I'm ver-y hard of hear-ing!

Speak a lit-tle loud-er sir, I'm ver-y hard of hear-ing!

2. Old Woman, Old Woman, are you fond of carding? (repeat)
   Speak a little louder, sir, I'm very hard of hearing! (repeat)

3. Old Woman, Old Woman, don't you want me to court you? (repeat)
   Speak a little louder, sir, I just began to hear you! (repeat)

4. Old Woman, Old Woman, don't you want to marry me? (repeat)
   Lawd, have mercy on my soul, I think that now I hear you! (repeat)

Play and Play Piano Book for Beginners

Color the pictures of the old woman and the young man.

BASS CLEF

TEACHER INSTRUCTIONS

Objects Needed

- **Board or chart to draw music staff**
- **Red and black markers**

Draw music staff with line 4 red and line 5 heavier black.

Draw the Bass Clef sign at the beginning of the staff as shown in Figure 1 below. Name the Bass Clef sign and define it as a clef sign that wraps around line 4, which names *F* below Middle *C*. Describe line 4 as "Fire Engine Red" as a help for the *F* note name.

1.

Guide the students to develop an understanding that the Bass Clef names the notes from Middle *C* on down the keyboard to the left and that the left hand will play the notes.

Draw *F G A* and *A G F* on the staff as shown in Figures 2 and 3.

2.    3.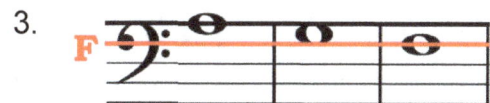

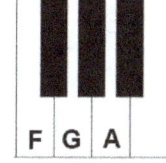

Play and sing the name names of the two patterns, left hand finger 5 on *F*.

Students play and sing the two patterns.

Guide the students to develop an understanding that the Bass Clef sign is different than the Treble Clef sign and that *F G A* are located differently.

PIANO/KEYBOARD INSTRUCTIONS

Students will follow the instructions as given in their student book.

Students will play familiar songs, *Hot Cross Buns*, *Frog in the Meadow*, and *Closet Key* in the Bass Clef. Model singing an octave higher as the students play the games and sing.

BASS CLEF

INSTRUCTIONS

Circle the Bass Clef sign below. The Bass Clef sign names the notes from Middle C on down the keyboard.

- The Bass Clef line 4 note name is **F**. The line is "Fire Engine Red" to help you remember **F**.
- The next note name going up the staff is **G**. It is above the **F** line and is in space 4.
- The next note name going up the staff is **A**. It is on the line 5 above the **G** space.

Find **F** on the keyboard with the fifth finger of your left hand. It is the F down to the left from Middle C. Your fourth finger will play **G** and your third finger will play **A**.

Play **F G A.**

Play **A G F.**

Circle the Bass Clef sign on the staff below.
Put finger 5 on F. Finger 4 will play G and finger 3 will play A.
The stems of the notes are going down to tell you to play with your left hand.
Play and sing the note names.

HOT CROSS BUNS

INSTRUCTIONS
Clap and read the rhythm.
Put your left hand finger 3 on A. Finger 4 will play G and finger 5 will play F.
Play and sing the letter names then play and sing the words.

Hot cross buns,   Hot cross buns,

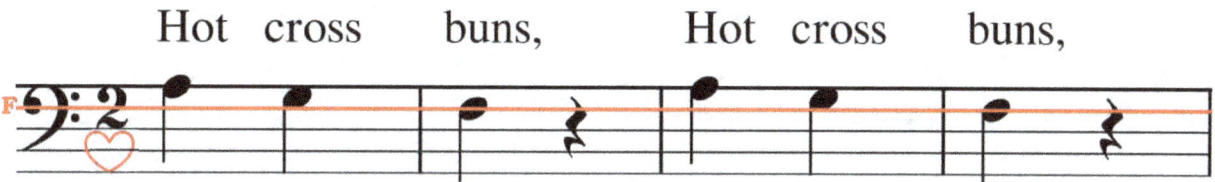

One a pen-ny, two a pen-ny, Hot cross buns.

Play and Play Piano Book for Beginners

FROG IN THE MEADOW

INSTRUCTIONS
Clap and read the rhythm.
Put your left hand finger 3 on A. Finger 4 will play G and finger 5 will play F.
Play and sing the letter names then play and sing the words.

Frog in the mea-dow, Can't get him out.

Take a lit-tle stick and stir him a - bout.

CLOSET KEY

INSTRUCTIONS
Clap and read the rhythm.
Put your left hand finger 3 on A. Finger 4 will play G and finger 5 will play F.
Play and sing the letter names then play and sing the words.

I have lost the clos-et key in that lad-y's gar - den,

I have lost the clos-et key, in that lad-y's gar - den.

COBBLER, COBBLER

TEACHER INSTRUCTIONS
Sing the song and play the game before students read and play the music on the piano/keyboard.

GAME DIRECTIONS
Object needed
- Xylophone mallet or small toy hammer
- *Cobbler, Cobbler* music on chart to tape to bottom of shoes
- Chair to represent cobbler's bench

Define the term, cobbler: one who works on shoes. Tape the first four measures of the song to the bottom of your left shoe and the next four measures to the right shoe. Sing the song and tap all the notes.

Story: *The cobbler stays very busy in the village, mending shoes. He had a pattern that he put on the soles of the shoes to be sure that he was repairing them correctly.* (Sing the song as you tap the bottom of each of your shoes to the rhythm of the song.) *He was so busy that he could not even take time for a coffee break.* (Sing song and tap rhythm on your shoes again.) *One day a child just your age from the village came in to have his (her) shoes mended. He needed them done by half past two. The cobbler said, "I just don't have time to mend your shoes by that time. You will just have to come back at half past four." When the child returned at half past four, the cobbler still had not repaired his shoes. The cobbler said, "Oh dear, I've been too busy! I know you need your shoes. I've got an idea! I will teach you how to mend your own shoes. Sit here on the cobbler's bench and I will give you a mallet. Tap the bottom of your shoes just like this.* (Have student sit in chair, attach music to soles of shoes; they sing and tap.) *Then the cobbler said, "You are doing a great job. I notice that you are following the pattern. Tap again and sing the pattern which is the bass clef note names."* (Student taps the rhythm of the song again, singing the note names instead of the words.)

PIANO/KEYBOARD INSTRUCTIONS
This song incorporates Middle *C* with the Bass Clef notes *A* and *G*. Draw the notes on the Bass Clef below. Guide students to develop an understanding that Middle *C* looks the same with the ledger line but that the location is above the staff in the Bass Clef.
Students will play and sing the note names.

Students will follow the instructions to the song as given in their student book.

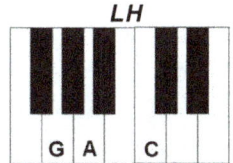

COBBLER, COBBLER

INSTRUCTIONS
Clap and read the rhythm.
Put your left hand thumb on Middle C.
Finger 3 will play A and finger 4 will play G.
Play and sing the note names then play and sing the words.

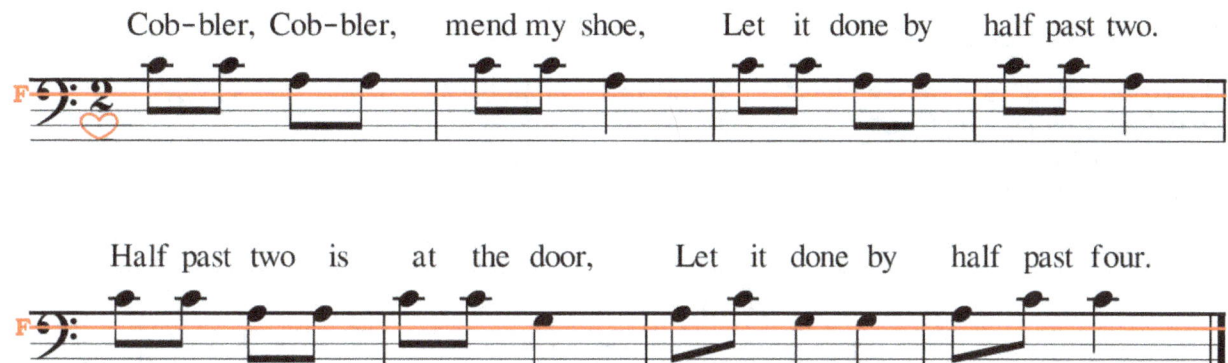

Play and Play Piano Book for Beginners

BASS CLEF B

INSTRUCTIONS
Objects Needed
   Board or chart to draw music staff
   Red and black markers

Draw known Bass Clef note patterns as shown in Figures 1 and 2. Play and sing the note names.

1.

2.

Draw Bass Clef B as shown in Figure 3. Name its location as sitting in the space above A, line 5.
Guide the students to compare its location to Middle C and A.
Draw the note patterns as show in Figures 4 and 5. Play and sing the note names.
Students will play and sing the note names.

3.

4.

5.

PIANO/KEYBOARD INSTRUCTIONS
Students will follow the instructions as given in their student book.

Teacher's Edition

FROG IN THE MEADOW

CLOSET KEY

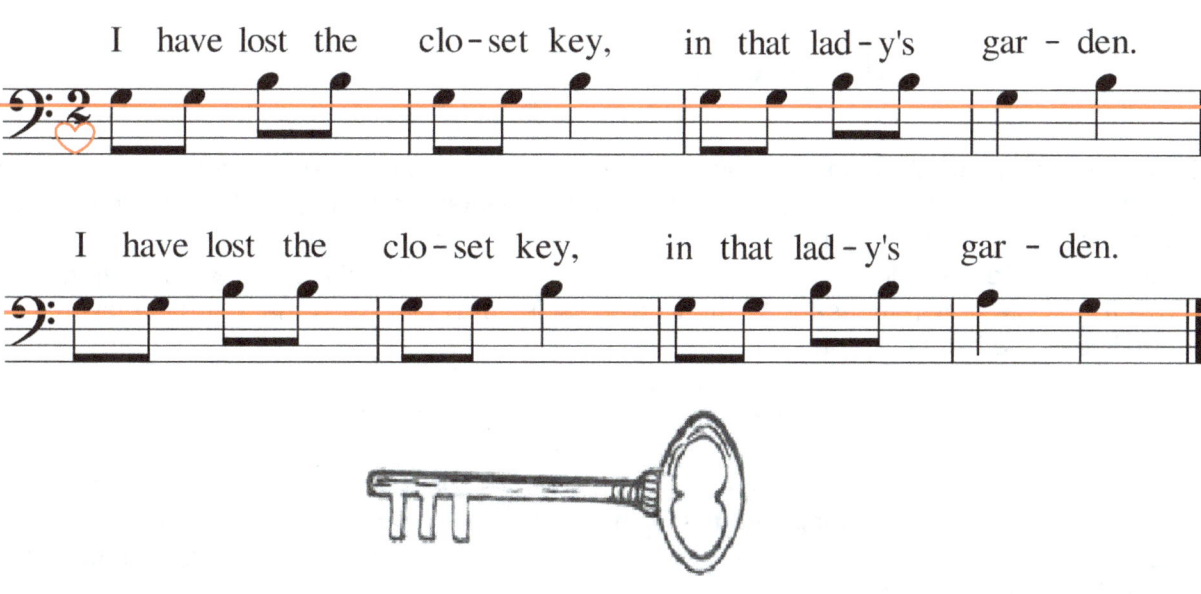

Play and Play Piano Book for Beginners

HOGS IN THE CORNFIELD
GRAND STAFF
WHOLE REST

TEACHER INSTRUCTIONS
Sing the song and play the game before students read and play the music on the piano/keyboard.

GAME DIRECTIONS
Objects Needed
- Rope, such as a small jump rope
- Ribbon
- Blue Painters Tape

This is tug-of-war game. Two students each hold one end of the rope. The ribbon is tied in the middle of the rope and is lined up directly above a strip of tape on the floor. Sing the song as the two students stand still. At the end of the song, the students try to move the ribbon to their side of the line as they pull. The winner is the first one to pull the ribbon to his/her side.

Alternate tug-of-war version: Two students stand facing each other on opposite sides of the tape, holding both hands with each other. At the end of the song, the students try to pull each other across to their side of the tape. **Caution: remind students to stop pulling whenever the other student gets over the line.**

PIANO/KEYBOARD INSTRUCTIONS
This song is an introduction to the Grand Staff. Define Grand Staff as the treble staff joined to the bass staff by a brace on the left with the treble clef on top.
Draw the Grand Staff. Circle the treble clef sign, bass clef sign and the brace.

Circle the meter signature on the grand staff. Guide the students to develop an understanding that both the treble clef and bass clef must have two beats per measure. If there are no notes in the song to play and sing, then a rest music symbol must be shown.
Circle the quarter rests in measure 2 and review that it takes the place of a ta, or quarter note. Circle the whole rest in measure 1. The whole rest is small black box that hangs below the fourth line of the bass or treble clef.

Define whole rest as a rest that means to rest for the whole measure.

Students will touch the notes and sing *Hogs in the Cornfield.* Guide the students to develop an understanding that music reading on the grand staff means reading from left to right in each measure and that in this song they will read treble clef notes and bass clef notes left to right within the same measure.

Students will follow the instructions to the song as given in their student book.

102 Teacher's Edition

HOGS IN THE CORNFIELD

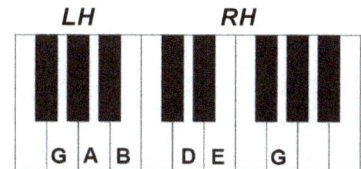

INSTRUCTIONS
Number the measures.
Sing the words and clap the rhythm.
Sing the rhythm names as you clap.
Put both thumbs on Middle C. Remember, the song begins at measure 1 in the Bass Clef.

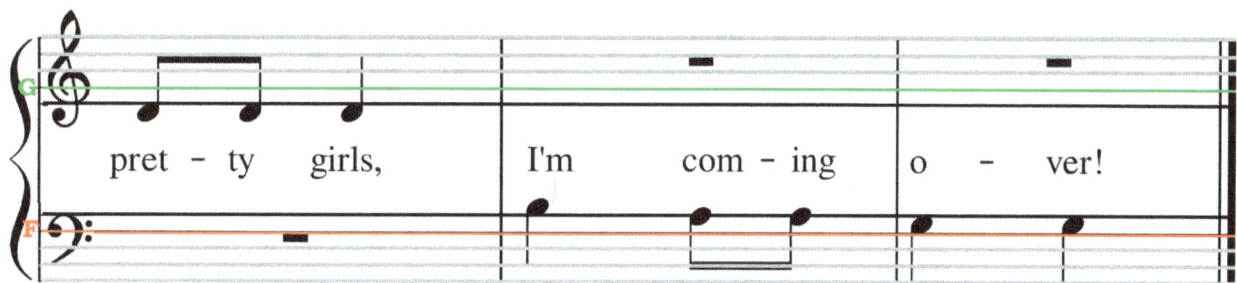

Play and Play Piano Book for Beginners

GRAND STAFF WRITING ACTIVITY

TEACHER INSTRUCTIONS

Copy the story for each student. Guide the students to observe the clef signs as they fill in the blanks. Be sure to have the ingredients on hand and enjoy an ice cream soda with your students!

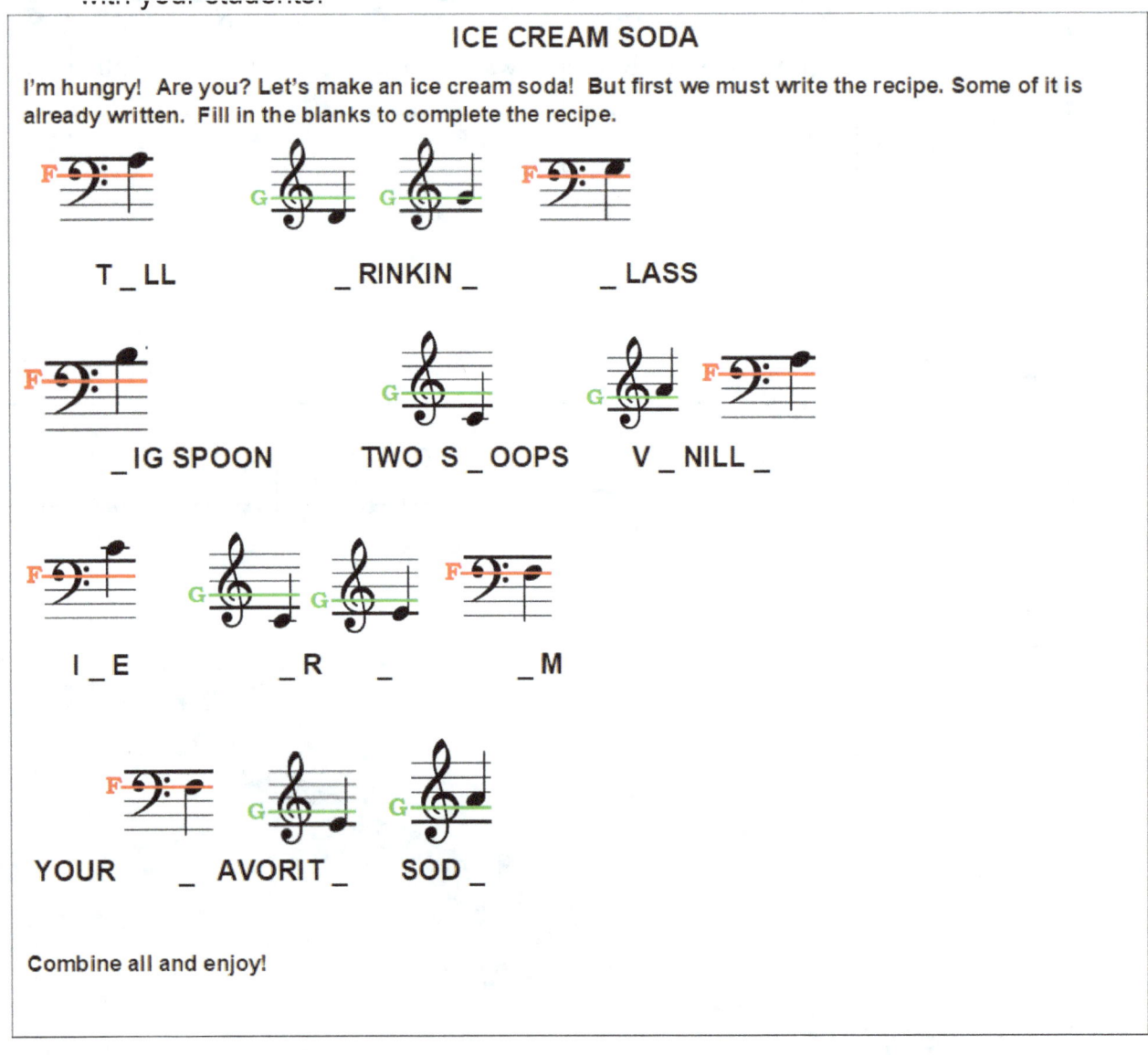

4 BEAT METER

HALF REST AND WHOLE REST

Sing the song and play the game to OVER THE RIVER TO FEED MY SHEEP, pages 106-107 before the students read and play the music on the piano/keyboard.

TEACHER INSTRUCTIONS

Objects Needed

- **Board or chart to draw music staff**
- **Black, Green, and Red markers**

Draw the beginning of the Grand Staff with the meter signature as shown in Figure 1.

1.

Lead the students to discover:

- There are two numbers in the meter signature on each staff called 4 beat meter.
- The top number is the counting number and counts 4 beats per measure.
- The bottom number is a symbol of the quarter note, called *ta*.
- The bottom number indicates that the quarter note, *ta*, gets one beat.

Draw the Half Rest symbol as shown in Figure 2 and the Whole Rest as shown in Figure 3.

2.   3.

Draw the first two measures of music to OVER THE RIVER TO FEED MY SHEEP as shown in Figure 4.

4.

Lead the students to discover:

- The Half Rest is the small black box above the third line on the staff. It takes 2 beats in 4 beat meter.
- The Whole Rest is the small black box sitting below the fourth line on the staff. It is a symbol to rest for the whole measure, which is 4 beats in the song.

Guide the students to count 4 beats on each staff.

Students will follow the instructions as given on their song sheet.

OVER THE RIVER TO FEED MY SHEEP

TEACHER INSTRUCTIONS Sing the song and play the game before the students read and play the music on the piano/keyboard.

GAME/DANCE INSTRUCTIONS:
Long ways set formation: 2 lines made up of partners facing each other in the opposite line.

```
"Charlie", head  x            o partner
                 x            o
                 x            o
                 x            o
           foot            foot
```

PHRASE	MOVEMENT
Over the river to feed my sheep	Step to center 4 beats
Over the river to Charlie	Step back to place 4 beats
Over the river to feed my sheep	Step to center 4 beats, join partner's right hand
To feed them well on barley.	Partners go around to change sides, drop hands and step backwards to change sides with partners, 4 beats
Tramplin' down the weavily wheat	Step to center 4 beats
Tramplin' down the barley	Step back to place 4 beats
Tramplin' down the weavily wheat	Step to center 4 beats, join partner's right hand
To bake a cake for Charlie.	Partners go around to change sides, drop hands and step backwards to original side, 4 beats
Charlie is a fine young man, Charlie is a dandy	Head "Charlie" makes up motion, going down the middle of the set, ending at the foot or end on the opposite side, 8 beats.
Charlie loves to go downtown To treat the girls to candy.	"Charlie's" partner goes down the middle of the set, imitating partner's motion, ending at the foot of the set on the opposite side, 8 beats.

Students will follow the instructions for the song as given in their student book, pages 58-59.

OVER THE RIVER TO FEED MY SHEEP

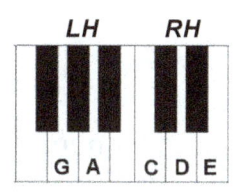

INSTRUCTIONS
Number the measures. Put both thumbs on Middle C.
Play and sing the rhythm then play and sing the words.

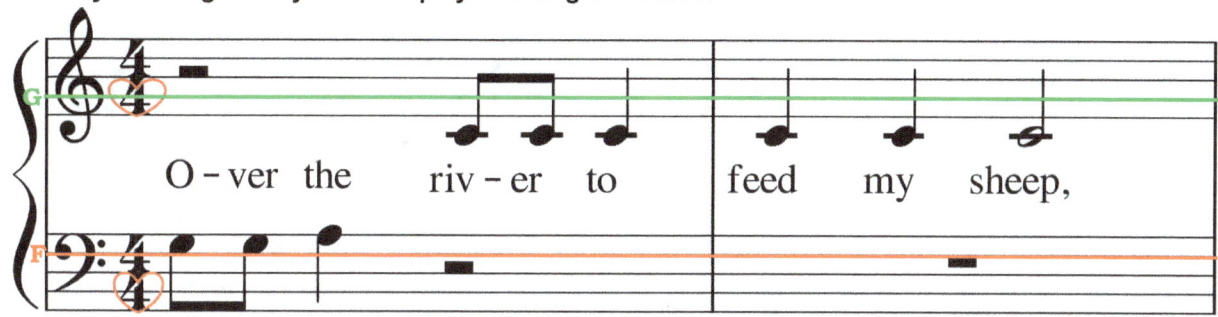

O-ver the riv-er to feed my sheep,

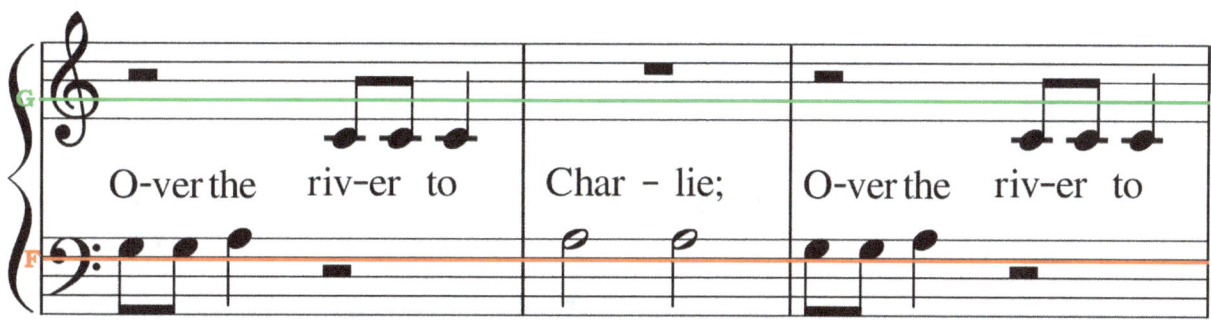

O-ver the riv-er to Char-lie; O-ver the riv-er to

feed my sheep, to feed them well on bar-ley.

2. Tramplin' down the weavily wheat, tramplin' down the barley,
   Tramplin' down the weavily wheat, to bake a cake for Charlie.

3. Charlie is a fine young man, Charlie is a dandy,
   Charlie loves to go dowtown to treat the girls to candy.

Play and Play Piano Book for Beginners

MUSIC SYMBOL MATCH

INSTRUCTIONS

Copy the worksheet below for each student.

Students draw a line to match each music term to its symbol as illustrated by number 1 on the worksheet.

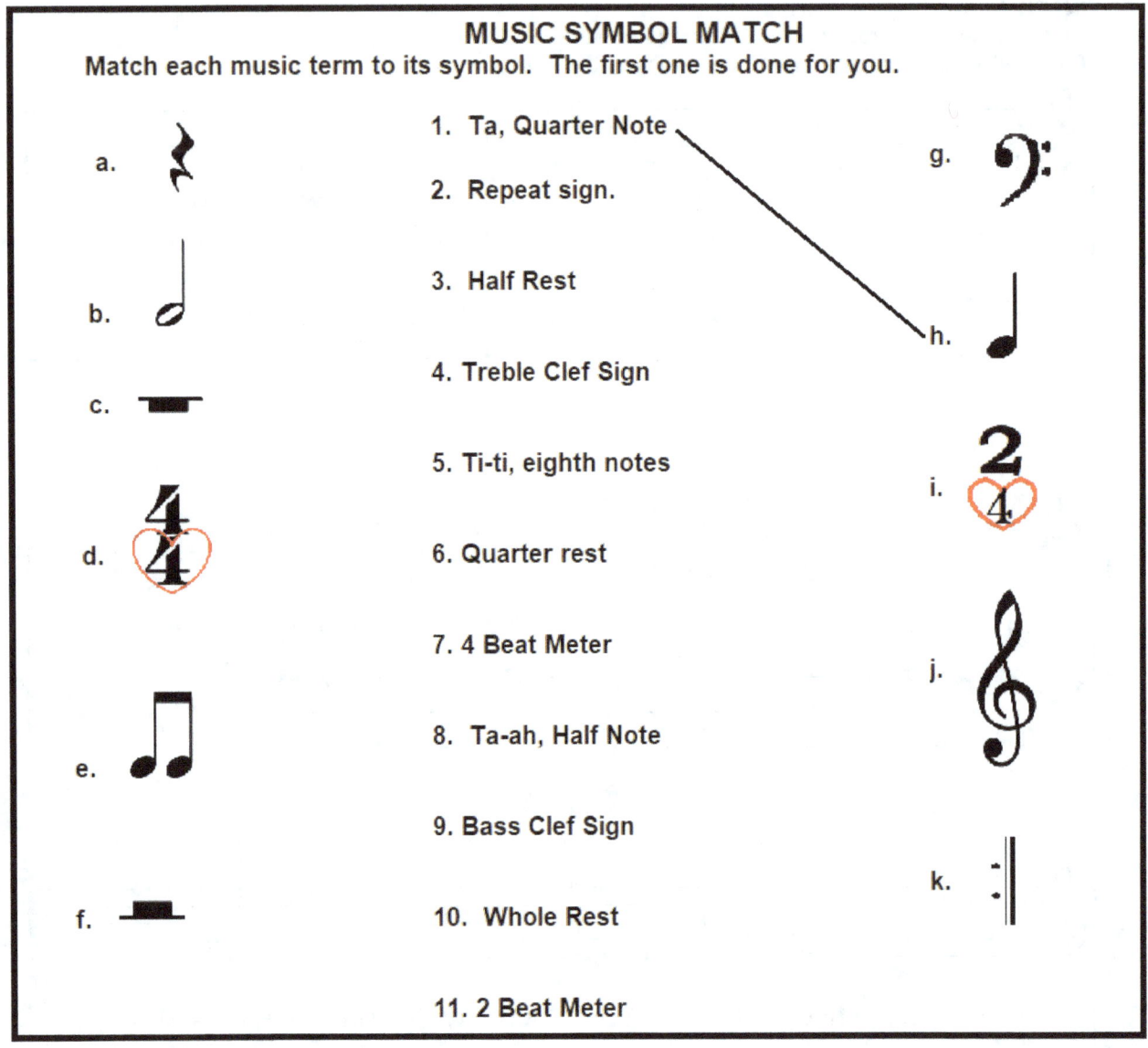

BOOTS OF SHINING LEATHER

TEACHER INSTRUCTIONS Sing the song and play the game/dance before the students read and play the music on the piano/keyboard.

GAME/DANCE DIRECTIONS
Circle formation, side step motion when circle right or circle left movement indicated.

Variation: Double circle formation for singing in two part canon.
Inside circle begins dance, outside circle begins after two or four beats in canon.

PHRASE	MOVEMENT
If you dance then you must have Boots of shining leather	Circle right, side step 8 beats
Money in your pocketbook, in your cap a feather	Circle left, side step 8 beats
But if you would sing with me	4 slow steps into middle of circle (half note value)
You don't need a cent, you see, So	4 slow steps out (half note value)
Come and sing together!	4 quick steps in place (quarter note value)
If you dance then you must have boots of shining leather!	Circle left, side step 8 beats
Oh!	Arms up

PIANO/KEYBOARD INSTRUCTIONS
This song uses the three rests the students have learned:

    Quarter rest   Half Rest   Whole Rest

Guide the students to name the rests found in measure 1 and in measures 5 and 6.

Students will follow the instructions as given on their song sheet.

Play and Play Piano Book for Beginners

BOOTS OF SHINING LEATHER

INSTRUCTIONS
Number the measures.
Put both thumbs on Middle C. Finger 5 of your right hand will stretch
  to play both A and B.
Play and sing the note names, then play and sing the words.
Play the song in a round with your teacher or another student.

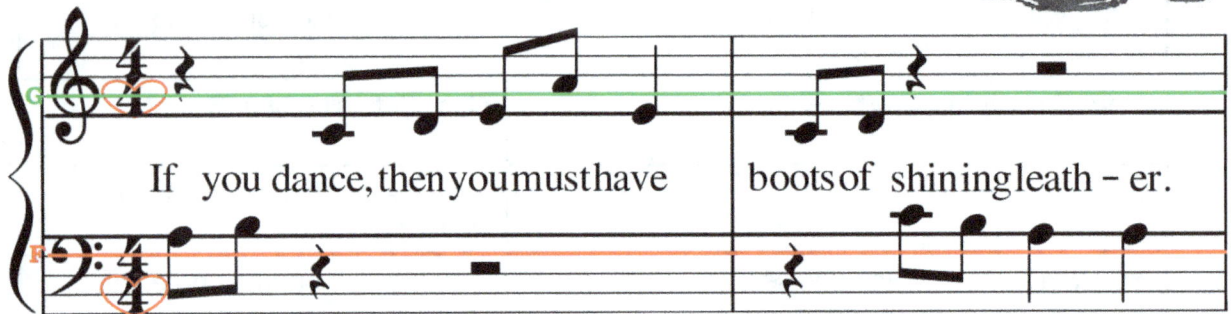

If you dance, then you must have boots of shining leath-er.

Mon-ey in your pock-et-book, In your cap a feath-er.

But if you would sing with me, You don't need a

Teacher's Edition

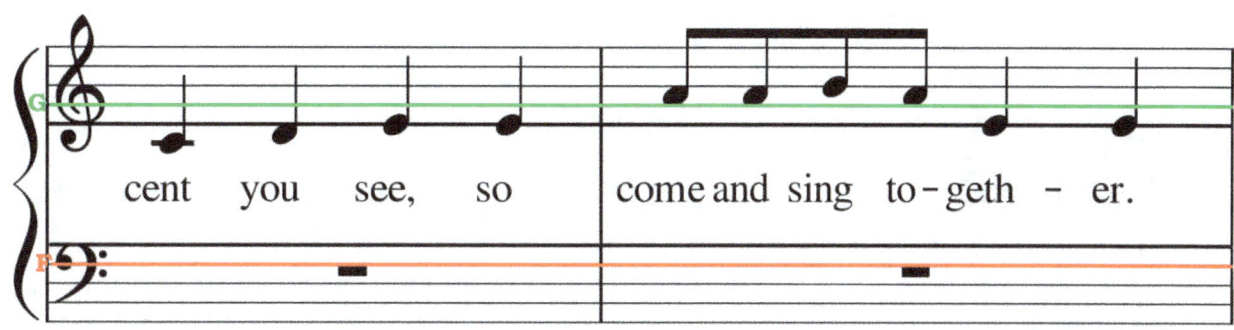

cent you see, so come and sing to-geth - er.

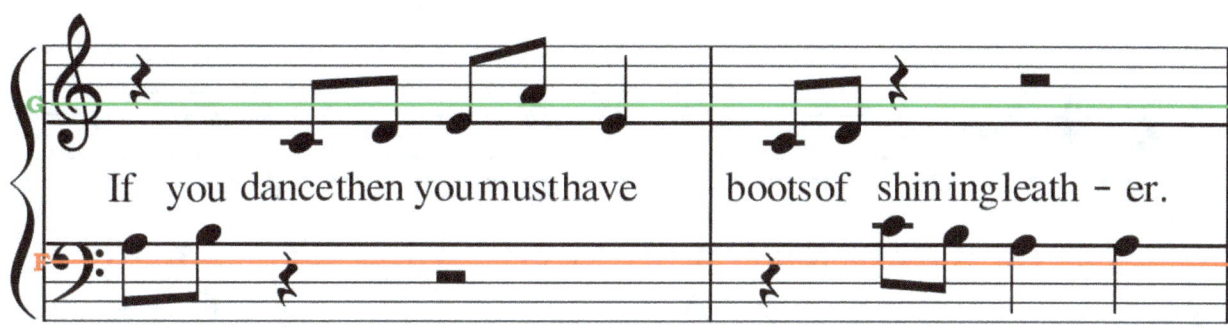

If you dance then you must have boots of shining leath - er.

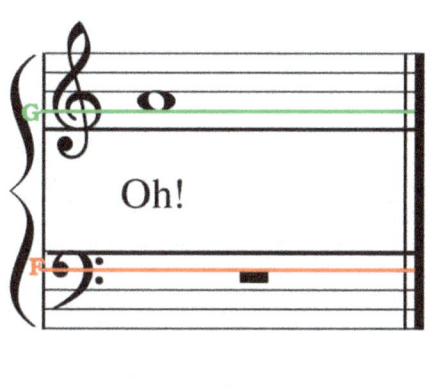

Oh!

BUTTON, YOU MUST WANDER

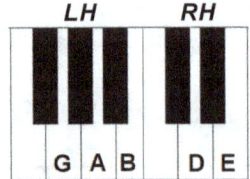

INSTRUCTIONS
Here is an old song to play on the Grand Staff.
Number the measures.
Put your Left Hand third finger on G. Put your Right Hand thumb on D.
Play and sing the note names, then play and sing the words.

3

Teacher's Edition

SPLIT TI (SINGLE EIGHTH NOTES)
KING'S LAND

TEACHER INSTRUCTIONS
Sing and play the game to this familiar song. Game instructions are found on page 80.

PIANO/KEYBOARD INSTRUCTIONS

Draw Figure 1 and Figure 2 on the board.

Define the notes in Figure 2 as single ti's. The beam joining the notes in Figure 1 is split to form two single ti's. Instruct the students that the notes are read exactly the same, *"ti-ti."*

Instruct the students that the single ti's help to form musical sentences.
Write the words to the song along with the rhythm.
Students will clap the rhythm as they sing the song, then sing the rhythm names as they clap.

Students will circle the music phrases on the student page as illustrated below.

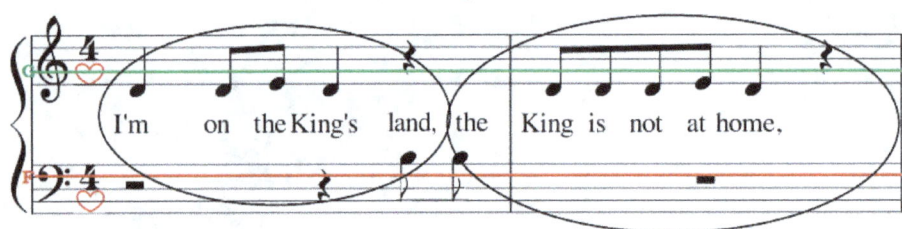

Students will follow instructions as given on their song sheet.

KING'S LAND

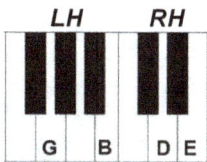

INSTRUCTIONS
Number the measures.
Circle the phrases in the words of the song.
Put both thumbs on Middle C.
Play and sing the rhythm names then play and sing the words.

I'm on the King's land, the King is not at home,

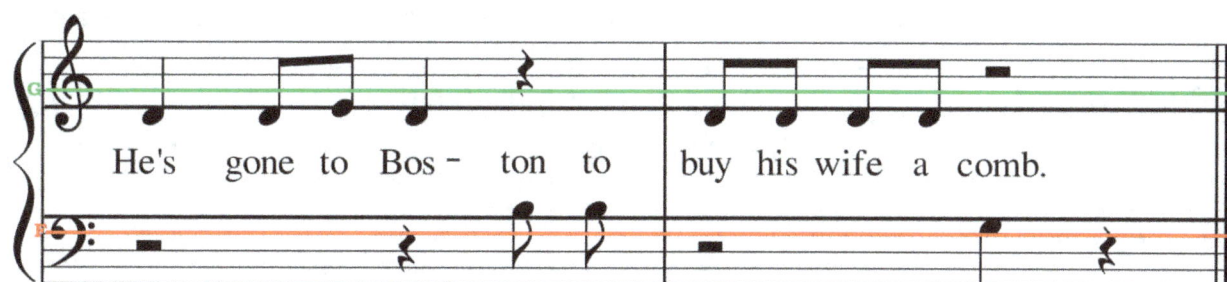

He's gone to Bos-ton to buy his wife a comb.

COME THROUGH 'NA HURRY
TI-TA-TI SYNCOPATED PATTERN

TEACHER INSTRUCTIONS
Sing the song and play the game before students read and play the music on the piano/keyboard.

GAME/DANCE INSTRUCTIONS:
Long ways set formation: 2 lines made up of partners facing each other in the opposite line.

```
head    x           o partner
        x           o
        x           o
foot    x           o partner
```

Dance Terms:
Sashay*: Head couple joins both hands in middle of set, gallops sideways to foot, then back
Cast Off**: Head couple turns outward from set and leads respective line down the outside of the set. Head couple meets at foot, forms an arch with both hands. Others in each line meet their partner at the foot, join hands, go under arch together, then back up to form lines. Head couple remains at foot and new head couple starts the dance again.

PHRASE	MOVEMENT
Come through 'na hurry, Come through 'na hurry	Head couple *sashays down middle of set to foot, 8 beats
Come through 'na hurry, Alabama Gal.	Head couple *sashays back to top of set, 8 beats
I don't know how, how, I don't know how, how	All partners step 4 beats to center of set then step 4 beats back to place
I don't know how, how, Alabama Gal.	All partners step to center, take partner's right hand to change sides, drop hands and step backwards to end on partner's opposite side, 8 beats
I'll show you how, how, I'll show you how, how	All partners step 4 beats to center of set then step 4 beats back to place
I'll show you how, how, Alabama Gal	All partners step to center, take partner's right hand to change sides, drop hands and step backwards to end on original side, 8 beats
Ain't I rock candy, Ain't I rock candy Ain't I rock candy, Alabama Gal.	Cast-Off**

Teacher's Edition

STAFF PAPER

TI-TA-TI PATTERN AND *TI* REST (EIGHTH REST)

MUSIC/KEYBOARD INSTRUCTIONS

Write the ostinato pattern as shown in Figure 1 below. *Ostinato* is a constantly repeated pattern.

Students sing verse 1 of *Come Through 'Na Hurry* and clap the ostinato pattern throughout the verse.

Students sing one phrase at a time and identify which word *(through)* takes 2 ti notes in each phrase.
Students identify on which single ti notes this occurs. (2nd and 3rd)

Tie the 2nd and 3rd single ti notes together as shown in Figure 2. (Review the tie music symbol from page 82.) Students will clap and read the rhythm.

Review: ♪ ♪ = ♡   ♩ = ♡   "Since ti-ti takes one beat and ta takes one beat, we replace the 2nd and 3rd tied single ti notes with one ta." Figure 3.

Students will clap and read the rhythm in Figure 3 above and the staff below.

𝄾 = ti rest (eighth rest)

Circle the ti rest (eighth rest). Guide students to develop an understanding that the ti rest takes the place of a single ti note.
Students will follow the instructions for the song as given in their student book.

COME THROUGH 'NA HURRY

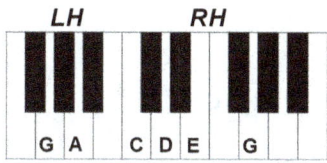

INSTRUCTIONS
Number the measures.
Circle the ti-ta-ti rhythm patterns in the song.
Circle the ti rests in measures 1 and 3.
Put both thumbs on Middle C.
Play and sing the rhythm names then play and sing the words.

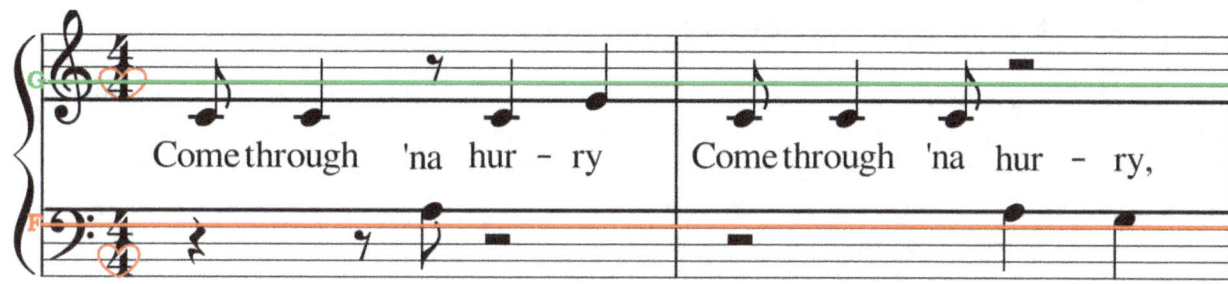

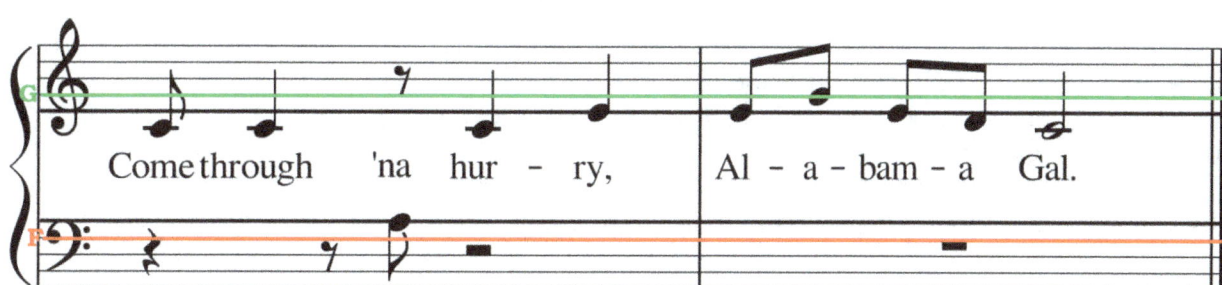

2. I don't know how, how,
   I don't know how, how,
   I don't know how, how,
   Alabama Gal.

3. I'll show you how, how,
   I'll show you how, how,
   I'll show you how, how,
   Alabama Gal.

4. Ain't I rock candy,
   Ain't I rock candy,
   Ain't I rock candy,
   Alabama Gal.

Play and Play Piano Book for Beginners

BIG FAT BISCUIT

TEACHER INSTRUCTIONS
Sing the song and play the game before students read and play the music on the piano/keyboard.

GAME DIRECTIONS
Objects Needed
Blue Painters Tape
Pencil, Pen or Marker for marking place on the blue tape

This is a standing broad jump game. Student stands at one end of the tape, feet together with toes at the end of the tape. As the song is sung, student bends knees and back up on the syllables "bah loo". On the last "bah loo", the student takes a standing broad jump on the tape. Draw a line on the blue tape and write student's initials wherever the back of the heel lands. Remind students this is a standing broad jump game and the rule is that the heel of the back foot is where the jump is measured.

PIANO/KEYBOARD INSTRUCTIONS
This song introduces the *tam-ti* rhythm (dotted quarter note followed by eighth note).

Have the students touch the notes and sing the song.
The students will circle all of the F# in the song then practice playing F#
on the piano/keyboard.

The students will follow instructions in their song sheet.

GRAND STAFF

Play and Play Piano Book for Beginners

TAM-TI RHYTHM
DOTTED QUARTER FOLLOWED BY EIGHTH NOTE PATTERN
BIG FAT BISCUIT

TEACHER INSTRUCTIONS
Write the rhythm pattern of Figure 1 on the board.

1.

Clap and sing the phrase, *"chew bah loo"* of the song, *Big Fat Biscuit*.
Compare the phrase to the rhythm pattern. Guide the students to discover on which part of the rhythm pattern the words occur.
Write the words under the rhythm pattern where the words occur, Figure 2.

2.
   Chew   Bah loo

Tie the ta to the first ti to make a longer sound, Figure 3. Students will clap the rhythm, holding hands together at the tie as they sing the words.

3.
   Chew   bah loo

Tell the students, "We will write the ta tied to the single ti using a short-cut, a dot. The dot takes the place of tie and the first single ti." Students will clap the new rhythm pattern and sing the words, Figure 4.

4.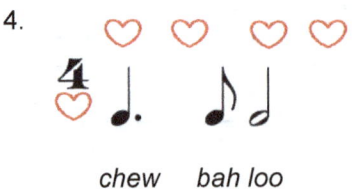
   chew   bah loo

Name the dotted quarter as *"tam"*, (pronounced "tahm"). The new rhythm pattern is read as *"tam-ti"*. (tam is pronounced "tahm"), Figure 5. Students will clap and read the pattern.

5.

Instruct the students that tam-ti equals two heartbeats.

Students will follow the instructions for the song as given in their student book.

Teacher's Edition

BIG FAT BISCUIT

INSTRUCTIONS
Number the measures.
Circle the tam-ti patterns.
Circle the ti-ta-ti pattern.
Circle the F#'s.
Put both thumbs on Middle C.
Play and sing the rhythm, then play and sing the words.

Big fat bis-cuit   chew bah loo.   Just from the o-ven,   chew bah loo, Boy

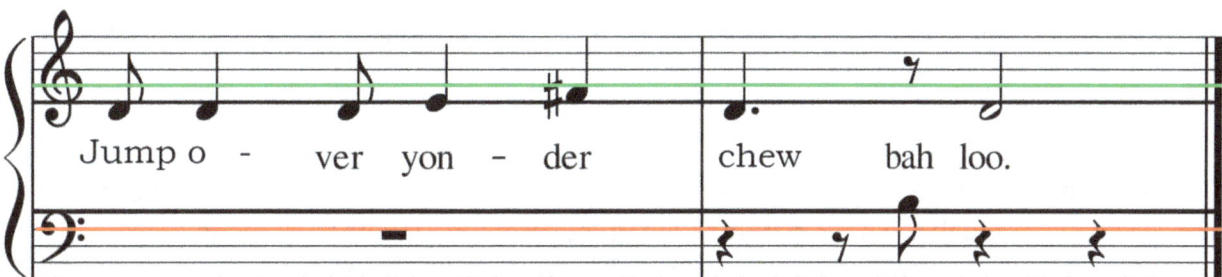

Jump o - ver yon - der   chew   bah   loo.

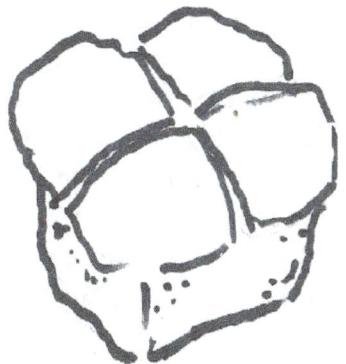

Play and Play Piano Book for Beginners

LONG ROAD OF IRON

TEACHER INSTRUCTIONS
Sing the song and play the game before students read and play the music on the piano/keyboard.

GAME DIRECTIONS
Object Needed
- Metal Soup spoons

This is a passing game. Students sit on the floor in a circle with legs crossed. Each student has a soup spoon on the floor in front of them with the bowl of the spoon faced down for easier grip to pick up the spoon. Practice the motions by chanting:

Pick – up, pass, pick – up, pass

On the words *"pick up"*, all the students pick up their spoon. On the word *"pass"*, they place the spoon on the floor in front of the person on their right. Continue this practice chant until the spoons are picked up and passed to the steady beat. Guide the students to keep the same motions on the steady beat so that each student picks up and passes the spoons on the same beat each time.

The students will sing the song and pass the spoons. The pickup beat at the beginning of the song is when they pick up the spoons to begin the passing game. Continue to pass the spoons throughout the song

Advanced game directions:
On the three beats of the words *"cheeky, cheeky chay"*, the students: 1. touch the floor in front of them, 2. touch the floor in front of the student on their left, then 3. pass the spoon to the person on their right. The song immediately begins again.

PIANO/KEYBOARD INSTRUCTIONS
This song introduces the incomplete measure. *Definition:* an incomplete measure at the beginning of a song is one that has less than the number of beats shown in the meter signature. The incomplete measure is always complemented by the incomplete measure at the very end. Guide the students to discover the beginning measure only has ti-ti, one heartbeat and the last measure has 3 heartbeats. The notes at the beginning incomplete measure are called anacrusis, or "pick-up" notes. Guide the students to begin numbering the measures at the first complete measure and that the pick-up notes in the first incomplete measure are part of the last measure to add up to the correct number of beats of the meter signature.

Students will follow the instructions for the song as given in their student book.

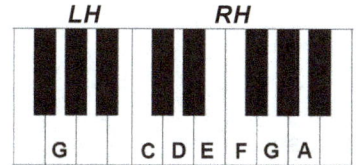

LONG ROAD OF IRON

INSTRUCTIONS
Number the measures. Look for the incomplete measure at the beginning of the song, then begin numbering after the barline.
Circle the tam-ti rhythms.
Put both thumbs on Middle C.
Play and sing the rhythm, then play and sing the words.

Oh, the | long road of i - ron, the | train to San-ta Fe, comes a

trav - lin' down the | track with a cheek-y, cheek-y | chay.

Play and Play Piano Book for Beginners

SKIP TO THE BARBER SHOP

TEACHER INSTRUCTIONS
Sing the song and play the game before students read and play the music on the piano/keyboard.

GAME DIRECTIONS
Objects Needed
- Hat or cap
- 3 bean bags
- 4 chairs
- Blue painters tape for boundary line
- Individually wrapped pieces of candy

Story: Someone just your age returned home from the barbershop. The child remembered he had forgotten his hat and 3 sticks of candy that the barber had given him. He skipped all the way back to the barbershop, picked up his hat and the 3 sticks of candy. He noticed an empty chair where he had sat. He also saw his friend sitting in a chair and Sister Sally sitting in another chair. He decided to share his candy. He tossed a piece of candy to his friend, one in the empty chair where he had sat, and one to Sister Sally.

GAME INSTRUCTIONS
The taped line is the beginning of the "barbershop". One chair is placed at the line to hold the hat/cap and 3 bean bags. The other 3 chairs are lined up in a row at a designated distance from the taped line. The student skips to the taped line, picks up the hat to hold in one hand and 3 bean bags in the other. The taped line should be such a distance from the 3 chairs to make it a challenge to toss the bean bags into the chairs. The bean bags are tossed one at a time on the words, *"one for you, one for me, and one for Sister Sally."*

Variation: Other students may sit in the chairs and try to catch the bean bags which are tossed. Also, real candy can be tossed.

PIANO/KEYBOARD INSTRUCTIONS

Students will follow the instructions for the song as given in their student book.

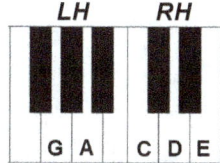

SKIP TO THE BARBER SHOP

INSTRUCTIONS
Number the measures.
Circle the ti-ta-ti pattern in the song.
Circle the tam-ti pattern in the song.
Put both thumbs on Middle C.
Play and sing the rhythm names then play and sing the words.

Skip, skip to the bar-ber shop, I left my hat at the

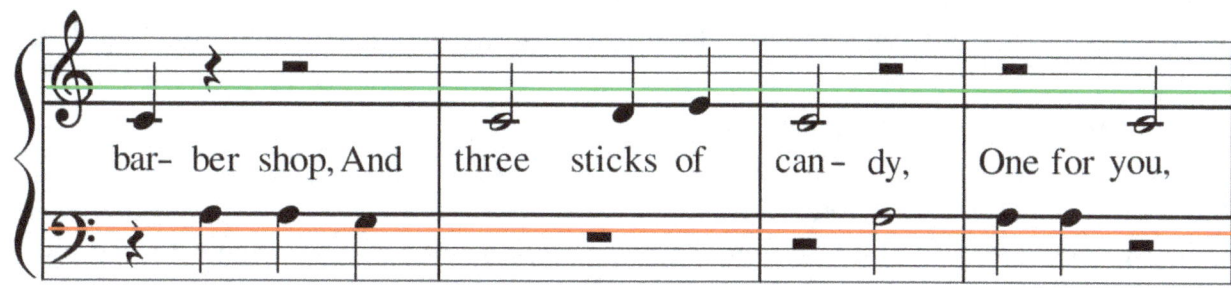

bar-ber shop, And three sticks of can-dy, One for you,

One for me And one for Sis-ter Sal-ly.

Play and Play Piano Book for Beginners

JUMP, FROG, JUMP
THREE BEAT METER

TEACHER INSTRUCTIONS

Sing the song and play the game before the students read and play the music on the piano/keyboard.

GAME DIRECTIONS

Objects Needed

- Alligator hand puppet or baseball glove to represent alligator's mouth
- Bean Bags for frogs
- Blue poster paper to represent water

Student 1 is the alligator and stands on the blue paper. Student 2 stands some distance from the alligator with a group of bean bag frogs nearby. The song is sung as student 2 tosses the bean bags one at a time into the water. The alligator tries to catch the frogs as they "jump" in the water.

PIANO/KEYBOARD INSTRUCTIONS

Draw the meter signature.

Instruct the students that this is a new meter signature and that there are three beats in each measure.

Sing the song and put the beat in three different places while singing:

- Pat knees
- Clap
- Snap fingers

The students will sing the song and put the beat in these three places.

The students will follow the instructions as given on their song sheet, student page 71.

JUMP, FROG, JUMP

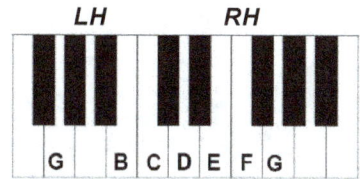

INSTRUCTIONS
Number the measures.
Circle the meter signature.
Put both thumbs on Middle C.
Play and count the rhythm. Remember to count 3 beats in each measure.
Play and sing the words.

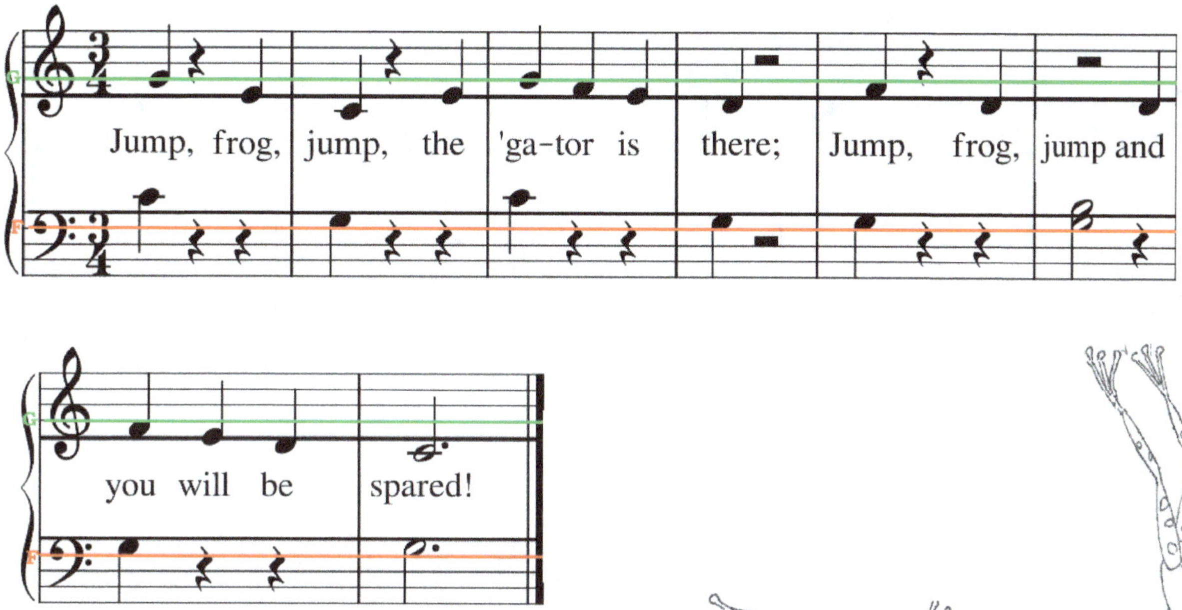

Jump, frog, jump, the 'ga-tor is there; Jump, frog, jump and you will be spared!

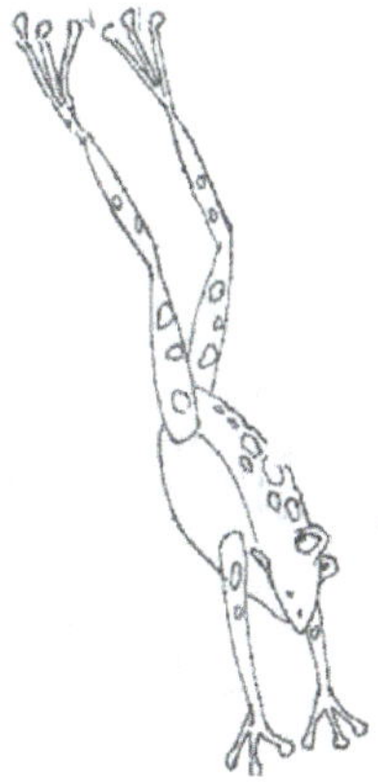

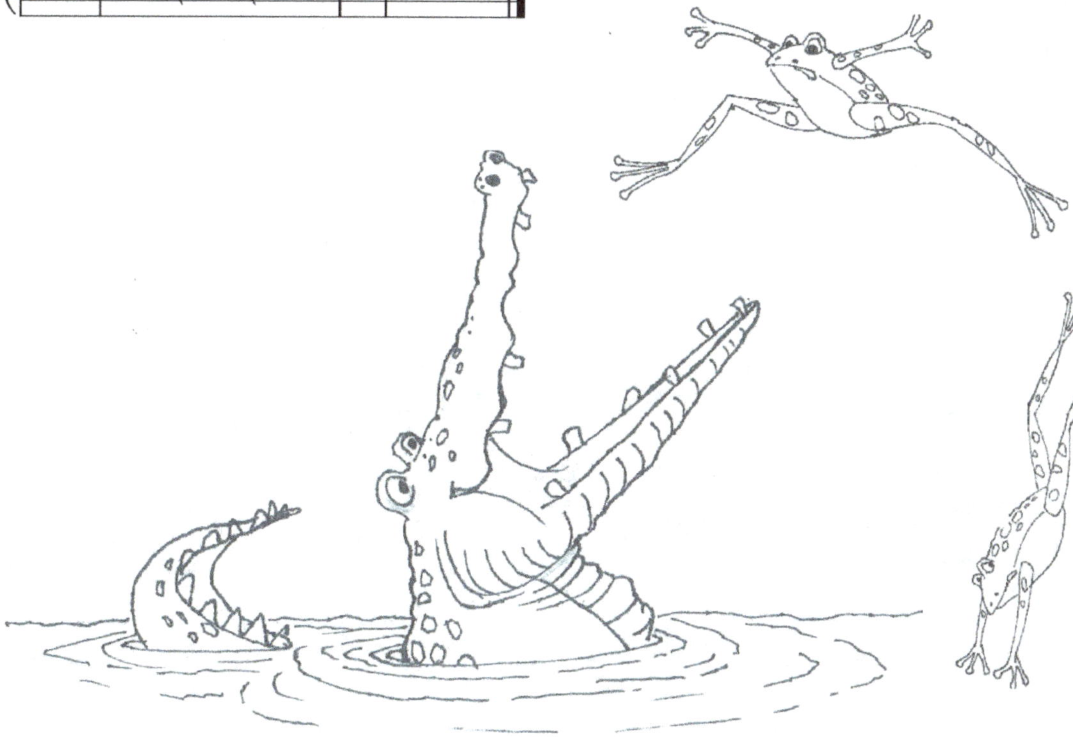

Play and Play Piano Book for Beginners

AMAZING GRACE

INSTRUCTIONS
Number the measures. Look for the incomplete measure at the beginning of the song then begin numbering after the bar line.
Circle the meter signature.
Circle the tam-ti rhythm patterns.
Play and sing the rhythm names then play and sing the words.

Teacher's Edition

TAM-TI 8 BEAT FLASHCARDS

Each student has a set of the 4 flashcards. Guide the students to discover that there are two 4-beat measures per card.
Suggested activities for the flashcards:
   *Students clap and read each card as instructed by the teacher.
   *Students put the cards in a specific order as instructed by the teacher. Students pat the heartbeat on their lap as they read the 4 cards without stopping.
   *Teacher claps and says a card. Students listen, echo clap and say the pattern then hold up the correct card.
   *Each student chooses a card to clap. Other students listen then hold up the the correct card. All students then read and clap the pattern together.

O COME, ALL YE FAITHFUL

INSTRUCTIONS
Number the measures. Look for the incomplete measure at the beginning of the song then begin numbering after the bar line.
Circle the meter signature.
Circle the tam-ti rhythm patterns.
Play and sing the rhythm names then play and sing the words.

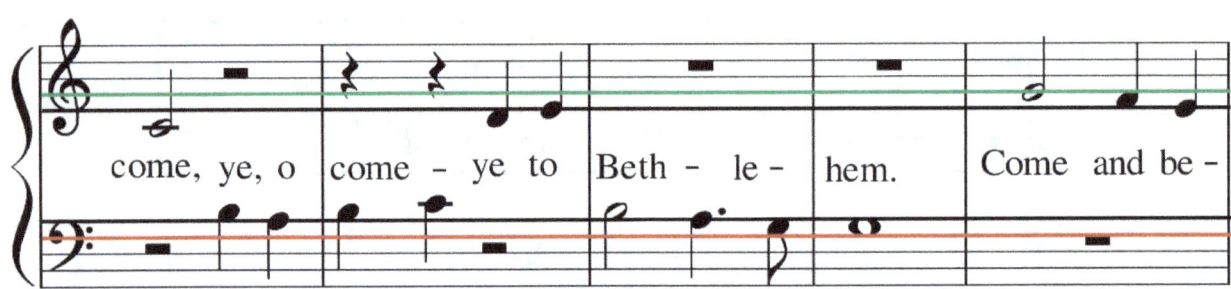

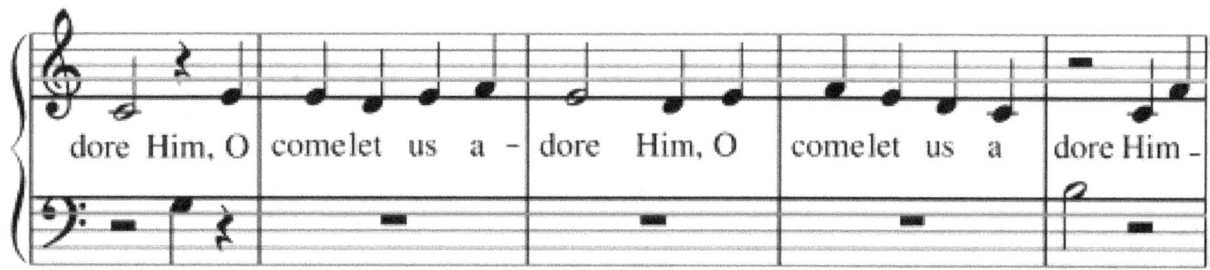
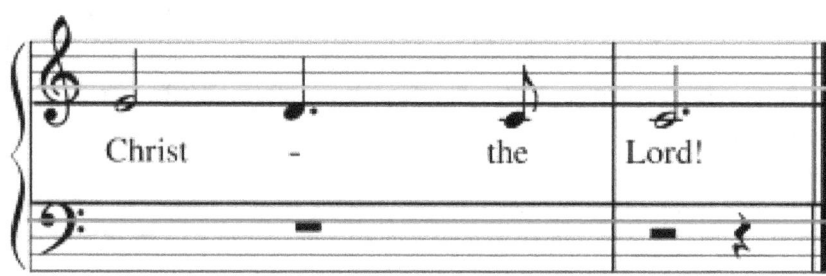

Alphabetical Listing of Pieces

Amazing Grace	130
Apple, Peach, Pear, Plum	18-19, 25
Bee, Bee Bumble Bee	26-27
Big Fat Biscuit	120, 122-123
Boots of Shining Leather	109-111
Bounce High	16-17, 21, 51, 67
Button, You Must Wander	76-77, 112-113
Closet Key	30-31, 74, 97, 101
Cobbler, Cobbler	98-99
Come Through 'Na Hurry	116, 118-119
Daddy Shot a Bear	78-79
Doggie, Doggie	36-37, 43
Ducks and Geese	48-49
Frère Jacques	88
Frog in the Meadow	32-33, 68, 72, 96, 101
Handy Dandy	4-5
Hogs in the Cornfield	102-103
Hop Old Squirrel	69, 73
Hot Cross Buns	71, 95, 100
I Climbed Up the Apple Tree	6-7
In and Out	12-13, 38, 44, 66
Johnny's It	62-63
Jump, Frog, Jump	128-129
King's Land	80-81, 114-115
Lemonade	46-47, 64-65
Long Road of Iron	124-125
Lucy Locket	22-23, 52
Nanny Goat	60-61
Naughty Kitty Cat	82-83
O Come, All Ye Faithful	132-133
Old Woman	89-91
Over the River to Feed my Sheep	106-107
Pease Porridge Hot	28-29
Plainsies, Clapsies	54-55, 67
Rain, Rain	20, 24, 42
Ring Around the Rosie	84-85
Skip to the Barber Shop	126-127
Snail, Snail	14-15
We Are Dancing in the Forest	56-57
Who's That Tapping at the Window	86-87

www.ingramcontent.com/pod-product-compliance
Lightning Source LLC
Chambersburg PA
CBHW081159070526
44583CB00021B/2917